SLAYING THE VAMPIRES, WEREWOLVES AND DEMONS OF INEFFECTIVE LEADERSHIP

EXPLORING EFFECTIVE LEADERSHIP PRACTICES THROUGH POPULAR CULTURE

Series editor: Michael J. Urick

The aim of this series is to examine modern and innovative business theories and methods via relatable popular cultural themes. The books will provide academically rigorous and credible applications and solutions to practitioners and upper level business students, in a format designed to be highly engaging and effective.

Swift Leadership: A Taylor-made Approach to Influence and Decision Making
Mariah Yates and Michael J. Urick

Leaders of the Caribbean: Lead by the Code
Pelin Kohn and Michael J. Urick

Forthcoming
Vaulting Over Adversity: Leadership Lessons from Simone Biles
John D Egan and Olivia Egan

SLAYING THE VAMPIRES, WEREWOLVES AND DEMONS OF INEFFECTIVE LEADERSHIP

By

Aditya Simha
University of Wisconsin – Whitewater, USA

emerald
PUBLISHING

United Kingdom – North America – Japan
India – Malaysia – China

Emerald Publishing Limited
Emerald Publishing, Floor 5, Northspring, 21-23 Wellington Street, Leeds LS1 4DL.

First edition 2026

Reprints and permissions service
Contact: permissions@emeraldinsight.com

British Library Cataloguing in Publication Data
A catalogue record for this book is available from the British Library

ISBN: 978-1-83753-429-6 (Print)
ISBN: 978-1-83753-426-5 (Online)
ISBN: 978-1-83753-428-9 (Epub)

I dedicate this book to all the various Buffy Summerses, a.k.a. Vampire Slayers in my life. You have all been so incredibly supportive and protective of me. I love you all!

CONTENTS

ABOUT THE AUTHOR

Aditya Simha is a Professor of Management at the University of Wisconsin – Whitewater. He obtained his PhD in Business Administration at Washington State University He teaches Leadership and Organizational Behavior at the MBA and Undergraduate levels, and teaches Micro Issues in Business, and Contemporary Research Methods at the Doctoral level. He has published articles in leading business journals such as the Academy of Management Perspectives, Journal of Business Ethics, and Group & Organization Management. He serves on the editorial boards of Management Decision and Journal of Business Ethics. He has published two other leadership books, one based on Harry Potter, and the other on Dogs. In addition to his many journal articles, he has published Leadership Insights for Wizards and Witches in the Exploring Effective Leadership through Popular Culture book series. He is passionate about a variety of pop-culture series and dogs. He lives in Waunakee (the only Waunakee in the Whole Wide World), Wisconsin, along with his wife and two young sons (ages 11 and 9). Until recently, they also had a beautiful beloved Otterhound named Fiona, who passed away on April 2, 2025.

ACKNOWLEDGMENTS

I have many people to thank and acknowledge here. It is safe to state that without these individuals, this book may have never seen the light of day and would instead be buried in a dark crypt with not even a single Turok-Han for company. First of all, I would like to thank my lovely wife Yasaswini and my splendiferous kids Advitiya and Ajinkya for being awesome! I would also like to thank my parents (Anand & Bhramara) and my in-laws (Sekher & Uma) for being fantastic parental figures. I also want to thank my dear older sister Aparna for being a fantastic Buffy'esque figure to my Dawn-like self (well, you get the idea).

I also thank my awesome series editor Dr. Michael Urick and the best Books Commissioning agents of all time, Daniel Ridge and Fiona Allison. I would especially like to shout out a loud appreciative thank you to Fiona for being so amazingly patient with me and my many requests for extensions. Thanks also to all of the Emerald support staff (including Lydia and Hemavathi) for their help in making this book come to light.

And I must say that while I haven't met any of the actors or directors of BtVS yet, I do have all intentions to meet several of them at the next fan expo that I'm able to go attend. I want to especially thank Sarah Michelle Gellar, Allyson Hannigan, Nicholas Brendan, James Marsters, Anthony Head, Michele Trachtenberg, David Boreanaz, Charisma Carpenter, Emma Caulfield, Seth Green, Kristine Sutherland, Amber Benson, Eliza Dushku, Marc Blucas, Julie Benz, Juliet Landau, Danny Strong, Alexis Denisof, Mercedes McNab, Adam Busch, Tom Lenk, Armin Shimerman, D.B. Woodside, Harry Groener, and anyone else who played a part in BtVS. You've all been a huge part of my vicarious living through BtVS, and I'm really excited to see a new show set in the Buffyverse.

Finally, I must thank the creator of BtVS (Joss Whedon), for having created a masterpiece series, one that has been profoundly impactful to many people across the world. Thank you to all my supporters, friends, family, and well-wishers from the bottom of my crypt... I mean soul. I have enjoyed writing this book, and I trust you will enjoy reading it and find it a fun book.

1

HOW DOES BUFFY MATTER FOR LEADERSHIP?

YES, BUT ABOUT LEADERSHIP?

Before jumping into the subject of how does Buffy matter for leadership, I must at the very outset clarify the eternal question about leadership and baldly state that leadership does, indeed, matter.[1-4] Certainly, there are people with viewpoints out there who would vociferously argue that leadership does not matter, but not to make too fine a point of it, those viewpoints are as erroneous as a flat-Earther indubitably is. Without leadership (or followership), one would hardly ever get anything done, be it a personal or a professional or a societal or even a national matter. On a more facetious level, without leadership being important, this volume you're clutching in your hands would not exist either. It would be as if it got pierced by a spiky wooden object and hence crumbled into a pile of vampiric dust. Luckily for us, that is not the case – you and I and most folks know that leadership (and followership) are both important concepts that are deserving of further elucidation and understanding.

For the folks who may be having a Harmony'esque moment here, allow me to briefly present the myriad sources of proof about the importance of leadership. For starters, there are quite possibly many thousands of books on leadership, and a burgeoning number of books on followership. A simple search on DuckDuckGo or Google or one of the ubiquitous generative AI engines out there will reveal the many books out there in print and in eBook format. Ahem... you can even find a book written by yours truly, which is set in the magical world of Harry Potter[5] and is a volume in the

Emerald Publishing series on Effective Leadership Practices through Popular Culture.[6–11] We still have magic in this book, it's just a different flair and flavor of magic, but it is magic nevertheless, some of which may be obtained for a small princely sum at The Magic Box. And yes, lots of vampires and demons (and the odd werewolf or two) are also inherently present.

And then of course, we have the thousands of scholarly research articles out there that make a convincing case for why leadership and followership are both important concepts.[12–16] Indeed, one could state that leadership and followership are so intractably linked with one another that one hardly knows when one ends and the other begins, or vice versa. However, in this book, I will be focusing on the leadership element but will throw in a healthy mix of followership for good measure. After all, good leadership is beneficial for followers too. So, yes, leadership and followership both do matter. But let us sashay our way back to why exactly I decided to write this book using the backdrop of Buffy Summers, she of the Vampire Slaying variety.

With one book on leadership in a Harry Potter context[5] already under my belt, I thought about writing another book steeped in a pop-culture context which was not only influential in impacting my own leadership philosophy but also influential in a larger way. I mean to say, it would not be very meaningful or even interesting if I were to write a book on some obscure context. People do have to know what the pop-cultural context is about, and the answer came to me on a decidedly Sunny Day (rhymes with Sunnydale, after all). It had to be Buffy the Vampire Slayer, a show which punched above its weight in terms of impact,[17–19] and has been recognized as being one of the most influential pop-culture shows and, indeed, has even received a lot of scholarly attention by academics of various disciplinary backgrounds.[20–23]

Buffy the Vampire Slayer (BtVS) was one of the shows that I would religiously watch without fail during my teenage years. It was always a joy to spend a breezy 45 minutes watching the show, but of course, it was always an hour long with all kinds of cola and laundry detergent advertisements interspersed throughout. However, I didn't mind that at all, the various adventures and trials and tribulations of the Scooby Gang were well worth suffering through the incessant saccharine and soapy err...soppy detergent advertisements. The various characters in the show, be it the heroes and heroines, or the anti-heroes and anti-villains, or the pure villains, were all well written and memorable (yes, even the Trio comprising of Warren, Andrew, and Jonathan, were quite memorable, weren't they?). And one of the greatest aspects of Buffy the Vampire Slayer was the realism in it, even if you consider the supernatural element inherent in it. After all, even garden or crypt variety Vampires or Mok'Tagar Demons[24] have to wrest with strong emotions and upheavals in dealing with other people and beings.

Some might say that there is perhaps a lot more drama in BtVS than is realistically possible; to those, I say, have you truly lived life without that element of drama? Our lives are usually embroidered with plenty of drama, even if not tinged with a supernatural element – we deal with financial stress, emotional stress, and the stress of dealing with people, and all those stresses can interact with each other to create new combinations. So, the drama in BtVS ought to be familiar for anyone who's ever experienced some kind of stress or stressor in their lives. Another criticism people can make about the show is that there isn't a whole lot of ethnic diversity on the show and, indeed, that is something that would probably be addressed if the show were to have come out in today's era. But, the Buffyverse still does have diversity within its ranks, by showcasing strong primary characters who are queer, or hailing from dysfunctional families, or from lives of poverty. So yes, while the show could have been more diverse, in comparison to other shows existing at the time, BtVS does decently in terms of that yardstick.

So, to circle back to my point, I really do think that Buffy the Vampire Slayer and all of the various characters in the Buffyverse are excellent examples to use to explain leadership concepts to people. And that is exactly what this book will set out to do – the remaining part of this chapter will essentially be an introduction to what the rest of the chapters will involve. You can take a look at the various chapters, and if you like to read Chapter 8 first, and then come back to Chapter 3, and then languidly saunter to Chapter 11, etc. Of course, I do think it would be more beneficial for you to go from this chapter to the next, and then to the next, till you finish the book, but hey, if you like going from season 1 to 7 and then stop at season 3 before going to season 5, that's perfectly fine. The book will still make sense even if you read it in a non-linear or a non-sequential way, but I do recommend reading it in the traditional sequence. Just to belabor that point, I have seen the various seasons of BtVS multiple times (I may or may not have subsequently learned and used some of Spike's biting vocabulary on random people during the heady impetuous days of youth), but I always watched them in a linear fashion. It just makes a lot more sense to do so because while there are certain episodes that I really enjoy more than some others, it feels a lot more coherent to adhere to the linear sequence. So now, I will basically lay out the general schema of the book and provide you, that is, the discerning reader with the structure of the book.

STRUCTURE OF THE BOOK

Alright, so let's get started with laying out the structure of the book. This particular chapter is the introduction chapter, and as is the usual wont, that tends to be chapter numero uno (discerning BtVS fans will remember Buffy's numero uno rule when it pertains to vampires, namely not to invite blood sucking dead people into the home). But when it comes to laying out the structure of a book, one of course wishes to invite people regardless of living status into the book. So, here we go with the laying out of the schema so to speak.

Following the introductory first chapter, the next or second chapter which is titled *Power (and Leadership) and Persuasion* will take a powerful leap into how power and leadership are connected. I will discuss the various types of power and relate them to leadership effectiveness. I will also discuss the intertwining of persuasion and power as they relate to leadership effectiveness, in particular zooming in on how different forms of persuasion and influence can be used by leaders. I will illustrate these concepts by using several characters and incidents from the BtVS world. Since many of the lead characters of BtVS are female characters, this chapter will probably introduce many if not all of the pertinent characters. Anya may or may not make an appearance in this chapter, but you can bet that many others will. Well, perhaps Anya will too – after all, we don't wish to risk enraging one of the finest vengeance demons out there, do we?

The third chapter titled *Responsibility – Leaders must Walk a Slayer's Path* will take a gander at explaining and discussing a key charge that is typically placed on a leader's shoulders. That key charge is of course responsibility, and effective leaders understand that responsibility to the people and organizations they're leading is an inalienable duty asked of a leader. While it can be hard, and lonely, leaders should still walk the path. In many ways, it is akin to a journey that a Slayer has to take. I will illustrate and discuss this particular theme by using characters and incidents from the BtVS world; however, I do anticipate that this chapter will have a lot of Buffy in it and perhaps a significant modicum of Faith as well. Other characters may feature a bit too, but it should Dawn on most people that the topic itself behooves itself to a discussion about Slayers.

The fourth chapter titled *Effective Mentorship – A Gilesian (and Others) Approach* will focus on the somewhat much neglected topic of mentorship as it pertains to leadership. Few persons can get to an elevated leadership position in life without the aid of good mentors in their corner, who open doors and gates for the mentee. In the BtVS world, mentorship is best represented by Rupert Giles (maybe a wee bit with Wesley Wyndam-Pryce). Giles is the sort of mentor that any aspiring Slayer (or leader as the case may be) would kill for to avoid having to die for. In this chapter, I will discuss the importance of mentorship in allowing leaders to truly grow as leaders. As always, I will feature various characters (who could be said to be formal mentors from the BtVS world), including Giles, Wesley, and even Mayor Wilkins. Hey, even Principal Snyder would probably work as an example of a poor-quality mentor; every mentor does not after all possess a Midas touch when it comes to being effective.

The fifth chapter is titled *Angelus to Angel – (Heart and) Soul Matters* and this one will discuss the role of empathy in leadership. After all, what made Angel into such a compelling character was the fact that the evil vampire Angelus was cursed into possessing a soul and because of that turned into the brooding and much suffering Angel. That humanity came with a dose of empathy, which resulted in introspection turned into bitter regret. So, as the title of the chapter suggests, there will be plenty of Angel in this chapter; but the overarching aim of the chapter is to discuss empathy in leaders or as I would rather put it, the heart and soul of leadership.

The sixth chapter titled *Self-leadership: Cues from the Scooby Gang* is all about self-leadership, and as the title also suggests, several members of the Scooby Gang will be making entries into this chapter. Self-leadership basically can be said to be a good substitute for formal leadership, and there are several instances in BtVS, where there is no formal leader in many situations, and that forces the Scoobies to display high levels of self-leadership. I will discuss the concepts integral to self-leadership by using various characters and incidents from the BtVS world.

The seventh chapter titled *A Spikey Path to Leader Identity* will discuss and introduce concepts pertinent to leader identity. And as the spiky title suggests, everyone's favorite poet turned vampire, William the Bloody, will be dominantly covered in the chapter. Identity is an important aspect of a person's sense of self and that applies equally to both leaders and followers. Identity is a multifaceted construct, and everyone has multiple layers to their identity. In this chapter, I will discuss why exactly leaders (and followers) need to be aware of how their identity is perceived. As it is for the other chapters, I will illustrate these concepts of identity by using incidents and examples from BtVS.

After the Spikey chapter, we move to the eighth chapter titled *Resilience (or How to Prevent Getting Staked into Dust Permanently)*. This chapter will be all about guts, well not the bloodied or bloodying variety, but rather the ones associated with grit and courage. The ability to bounce back after defeat or lack of victory is what one associates with resilience, and this is something leaders (and Slayers) need to have in order to be effective. Remember the Xander quip from an episode where he likens himself to the cavalry, albeit a cavalry which is just the one scared individual (i.e., himself) armed with a rock. To me that is something resilient people do, they show up regardless of how doable a particular task is. They don't give up, and neither do resilient leaders. I will discuss resilience and use several examples and incidents from BtVS.

The ninth chapter which is titled *Revenge Versus Redemption – A Nay or Anya?* is going to be a discussion of themes centering on forgiveness. Leaders have a choice, they can be revengeful creatures, who end up giving contracts to vengeance demons. Alternatively, they can be open to forgiveness and help people achieve redemption. There are obviously pros and cons to either approach, and in this chapter, I will strive to explain what either course of action can mean for leaders (or followers too). As is the motif of the book, I will use examples of people from BtVS, and the various incidents they are involved in. Anya (and possibly Halfrek) will possibly make a sizeable appearance in this chapter for sure.

Passing on to the 10th chapter which follows and is titled *Followers Matter Too – Xander's X-factor*, I will focus my discussion on the general topic of followers. While this book is about leadership, without followers, leadership is pretty much a case of yin without yang or vice versa. While the chapter does refer to Xander (who can be arguably said to be an amazing follower), there are other characters from BtVS who have at times essayed follower roles and at times essayed leader roles. Sometimes, leaders have to follow, and followers have to lead; it's a delicate matter of knowing when to do what. I will explain this X-factor of sorts in this chapter while using various BtVS incidents and characters.

The 11th or the penultimate chapter titled *Willow Walk Alone? Leaders and Loneliness* will discuss the lonely path leaders must often traverse. It is entirely possible to be surrounded by hundreds of people, but yet feel lonely. After all, leaders have to make decisions and take action that they are wholly responsible for. That can mean that sometimes unpopular decisions are taken and that can exacerbate the loneliness. While Buffy herself often grappled with the loneliness that being a Slayer comes with, I think Willow also really exemplified that loneliness, especially when she became Dark Willow, after Tara's unfortunate incident involving Warren (spoiler perhaps, a bit, but the show is old enough that this is probably only a spoiler for someone who has never ever heard of Buffy, in which case, I doubt they're reading the book, so there's that). In this chapter, I will discuss and explain how loneliness ties in with leadership and how leaders need to tackle it. I will use and refer to various BtVS characters to do so.

And finally, the ultimate chapter or the 12th chapter arrives. This one is titled *Conclusion – How to Be the Quintessential Slayer*. In this chapter, I will basically sum up the essence of the book and provide the reader with a coherent idea of how they too can be an effective leader (or Slayer of ineffectiveness). This chapter will help readers get some solid takeaways on how to be a leader (or follower) who knows how to vanquish the various evils that befall effective leadership.

So, that is the intended layout of this book – I certainly do hope that the book will be interesting for the readers and that there will not be too many complaints going out to D'Hoffryn. And one of my primary goals from this project is to demonstrate (as several other books in the series have) that people can learn about leadership and followership from pop culture, regardless of the kind of pop culture being referred to. This applies even if you are watching a fictional series about a youthful young woman and her friends, and their adventures protecting the citizenry from various demons, zombies, vampires, and other creatures of various descriptions. I believe this book will be useful for individuals who would like to learn more about leadership and followership and be better leaders themselves. They may also pick up a bit of Giles' wry humor or Spike's witty insults, or Xander's indescribable metaphorizing, or even Buffy's quipping quotient. But that's just par for the course, isn't it? While, the book will be more enjoyable for folks well versed with the Buffyverse, I think even individuals who have none or just a passing familiarity with the Buffyverse will be able to understand and follow along with the book. And should they wish to dive in to the Buffyverse, that is an easy enough task to go find all the episodes or clips streaming or on DVD.

SUMMARY

This first chapter introduces the layout of the book and presents a short discussion of how exactly BtVS is a pertinent context to learn about and discuss leadership. In this chapter, I essentially aim to show how the upcoming chapters connect with or map on to leadership concepts. The next chapter takes a peek into power, gender, and leadership, and you'll get a peek into several of the BtVS characters.

REFERENCES

1. Jervis, R. (2013). Do leaders matter and how would we know? *Security Studies*, 22(2), 153–179.

2. Hackman, J. R., & Wageman, R. (2004). When and how team leaders matter. *Research in Organizational Behavior*, 26, 37–74.

3. Waldman, D. A., Ramirez, G. G., House, R. J., & Puranam, P. (2001). Does leadership matter? CEO leadership attributes and profitability under conditions of perceived environmental uncertainty. *Academy of Management Journal*, 44(1), 134–143.

4. Antonakis, J., Banks, G., Bastardoz, N., Cole, M., Day, D., Eagly, A., Epitropaki, O., Foti, R., Gardner, W., Haslam, A., Hogg, M., Kark, R., Lowe, K., Podsakoff, P., Spain, S., Stoker, J. I., Van Quaquebeke, N., Van Vugt, M., Vera, D., & Weber, R. (2019). The leadership quarterly: State of the journal. *The Leadership Quarterly*, 30(1), 1–9.

5. Simha, A. (2022). *Leadership insights for wizards and witches*. Emerald Publishing Limited.

6. Urick, M. J. (2021). *A manager's guide to using the force: Leadership lessons from a galaxy far far away*. Emerald Publishing Limited.

7. Urick, M. J. (2021). *Leadership in middle-earth: Theories and applications for organizations*. Emerald Publishing Limited.

8. Schmidt, G. B., & Islam, S. (2022). *Leaders assemble! Leadership in the MCU*. Emerald Publishing Limited.

9. Wildermuth, C. D. M. E. S. (2024). *Against all odds: Leadership and the handmaid's tale*. Emerald Publishing Limited.

10. Tong, N., & Urick, M. J. (2023). *Bend the knee or seize the throne: Leadership lessons from the seven kingdoms*. Emerald Publishing Limited.

11. Yost, K. (2024). *Courageous companions: Followership in doctor who*. Emerald Publishing Limited.

12. Haslam, S. A., & Platow, M. J. (2001). The link between leadership and followership: How affirming social identity translates vision into action. *Personality and Social Psychology Bulletin*, 27(11), 1469–1479.

13. Plachy, R. J., & Smunt, T. L. (2022). Rethinking managership, leadership, followership, and partnership. *Business Horizons*, 65(4), 401–411.

14. Matthews, S. H., Kelemen, T. K., & Bolino, M. C. (2021). How follower traits and cultural values influence the effects of leadership. *The Leadership Quarterly*, 32(1), 101497.

15. Ete, Z., Epitropaki, O., Zhou, Q., & Graham, L. (2022). Leader and organizational behavioral integrity and follower behavioral outcomes: The role of identification processes. *Journal of Business Ethics*, 176(4), 741–760.

16. Cai, D., Cai, Y., Sun, Y., Xu, R., & Feng, B. (2021). Leader-follower congruence in need for achievement and work outcomes: The mediating role of leader-member exchange. *Applied Psychology*, 70(4), 1492–1511.

17. Jarvis, C., & Burr, V. (2011). The transformative potential of popular television: The case of Buffy the Vampire Slayer. *Journal of Transformative Education*, 9(3), 165–182.

18. Mathams, N. (2023). *"A kindred spirit": The impact of Buffy the Vampire Slayer and the Vampire diaries on adolescent viewers* [Doctoral dissertation, Macquarie University].

19. Jarvis, C., & Burr, V. (2005). 'Friends are the family we choose for ourselves' Young people and families in the TV series Buffy the Vampire Slayer. *Young*, 13(3), 269–283.

20. Wilcox, R., & Lavery, D. (Eds.). (2002). *Fighting the forces: What's at stake in Buffy the Vampire Slayer*. Rowman & Littlefield.

21. Early, F. H. (2001). Staking her claim: Buffy the Vampire Slayer as transgressive woman warrior. *The Journal of Popular Culture*, 35(3), 11–27.

22. Davies, M. (2010). "You can't charge innocent people for saving their lives!" Work in Buffy the Vampire Slayer. *International Political Sociology*, 4(2), 178–195.

23. Richards, C. (2004). What are we? Adolescence, sex and intimacy in Buffy the Vampire Slayer. *Continuum*, 18(1), 121–137.

24. Fandom. (n.d.). *Mok'tagar demon*. Buffy the Vampire Slayer Wiki. Retrieved January 24, 2024, from https://buffy.fandom.com/wiki/Mok%27tagar_demon

2

POWER (AND LEADERSHIP)
AND PERSUASION

Power is an interesting word; to some, the word appears almost like it's been laced with a heaping of burning arsenic, while for others, it feels like it's been slathered with a delicious butter-cream topping of sorts. Basically, one can see power as being a negative construct, as in, people with powers can abuse them to harm others; or, one can see power as being a positive construct, as in, people with powers can use them to benefit others. The superheroes and supervillains concepts basically involve powers and constructive use or destructive abuse situations. When it comes to leaders though, generally speaking power is something that they do need to possess. For instance, one can hardly be expected to be a Slayer if one lacks the ability to actually slay vampires, right? And similarly, if you're rendered a powerless vampire (like Spike was with the chip in his head), life can be rather dreary since you're quite unable to function the way a normal vampire would. Ditto with leaders – if they lack power, they are just not going to be very effective leaders. There are obviously many ways to obtain power, some legitimate and ethical, while others are decidedly unethical. When you mix gender in to this equation, things get interesting, and power dynamics are certainly affected.

In this chapter, I will first begin by explaining how exactly one defines power and then will follow that with discussing the various bases of power. Following the power discussion, I will then pivot to how power matters when it comes to persuasion. In the BtVS world, various kinds of persuasion certainly come prominently into discussion, and therefore, I too will discuss them in conjunction with power and use suitable examples from BtVS to help cement understanding of these concepts. Let's embark on a power(ful) journey that should hopefully engender some deepish comprehension of how power is vital for leadership.

POWERING THROUGH THE BASES

As I mentioned previously, power basically comes charged with ability, by that I mean, that if someone has power, they have the ability to effect or resist change. A powerless person is more or less the equivalent of a human cork bobbing about in a tumultuous ocean of challenge. There are plenty of formal definitions of power, some of them imbued with the magical capability to put their readers into a sturdy stupor, but having said that, it is entirely possible to define power in an easy to comprehend way. As Dawn Summers would put it, it is, indeed, a "smellimentary" matter. An easy way to think about power is that it denotes a person or an entity's ability to influence others or to resist influence from others. It also comes with the ability to control people, control incentives, control decisions, and control resources. As you can tell, power is something that a majority of people would like to have (I say majority and not everyone because there's always some folks out there who claim that they do not crave or desire any kind of power).

Even in the Buffyverse, if you look at the various characters (especially the villain types), a lot of their villainy comes from this desire to increase their power or to avoid losing what power they have. Take Glory, for instance, or Glorificus if you're wanting to be formal – she had immense power on Earth, but that power was a mere shade of its former self. After Glory was evicted from her original Hell dimension thanks to two other gods (who conspicuously did not wish to share power with Glory), she was marooned on Earth with her essence trapped inside Ben Wilkinson. Glory desperately wanted to go back to her original dimension and sought out a magical energy nexus called the Key (this energy nexus was transformed into Buffy's sister Dawn by the Order of Dagon), which would have helped her to break down the barriers between various dimensions, and literally allow Hell to be recreated on Earth. But anyway, that's basically an explanation of power in an easy to digest nutshell. Let's move on to the bases of power next.

The original purveyors of the bases of power are two scholars named French and Raven, who envisaged their conceptualization of the bases of power back in 1959.[1] These sources are depicted with their name alongside the pertinent power. So, we have reward power, coercive power, legitimate power, expert power, and referent power.[2-4] Let's start off with reward power first, shall we? It's bound to be rewarding in its own way, you bet (as Buffy would put it!).

Reward power has to do with the ability of leaders to reward their subordinates and employees.[1-4] The purpose is to get people to do what you want because you can give the person something they like getting. In other words, it has to be a reward that the subordinate cares about. Reward power means nothing if the rewards being doled out are not attractive to the intended recipient. Consider for a moment that you have the ability to reward an individual with a truckload of Japanese Manga if that individual does something for you. That reward would work very well indeed if the intended recipient is a Manga enthusiast – however, for a non-enthusiast, the reward will not be very alluring. Think about someone like Rupert Giles – a reward like that would be decidedly unappealing for him. For the reward to be alluring for Giles, it would have to consist of a collection of historical and mystical artifacts. As a leader, you really do have to be able to offer rewards that are desirable, be it from a financial or extrinsic motivation standpoint or from an intrinsic motivation standpoint. If the reward meets neither category, then the reward is probably not going to result in influencing anyone much.

Moving along to coercive power[2,5,6] next – think of this as the antonym of reward power, or as the stick to the carrot that rewards are. Here leaders have coercive power if they are able to punish their followers for flouting their orders or requests. This punishment can take on many forms, some of which could be minor in scope, such as paying out fines or having to file for sick leave. Sometimes though, the punishment could be severe and could include drastic measures such as firing employees or demoting them. While coercive power seems like a great thing to have, it can have unintended consequences, such as employees/followers starting to resist the leader, due to the over-reliance on coercive power. So, leaders should treat this particular base of power with caution, unless you happen to be The Master (or Principal Snyder) who throw caution to the wind, and are quite ruthless with their use of coercive power.

The next base of power to discuss here is legitimate power.[2,7] This is the power that an individual has due to their formal ability to possess authority. So, a King or a Queen of a country, where the royalty has not been abolished, would be a good example of a person with legitimate power. A good example to use here in this context from BtVS is when Giles was fired by Quentin from the Watcher's Council. So, his legitimate power was eviscerated, and instead, that particular power, that is, the power of being the Slayer's Watcher, was bestowed on Wesley Wyndham-Pryce. In a later season (season 5 to be precise), Giles is reinstated as the official Watcher of Buffy's, as Wesley had gotten fired due to his mishandling of Faith Lehane (the secondary Slayer, stay with me here; she'll appear more in this book). So that Giles versus Wyndham-Pryce shuffle neatly demonstrates what legitimate power is about. It has to do with one's possessing formal authority, and it is a base of power that can be given or taken away. Now, let's jog along to a base of power that is a bit more difficult to be taken away.

Expertise power[2,8] is the base of power that I will discuss next. As the name signifies, it has to do with the expertise and skills and knowledge that a person has, that allows them to use it in ways that are beneficial for tasks and goals. You have expertise power in a certain area if you are the individual who is recognized as possessing the most relevant or effective skills for a given task or a given area. Let's imagine that you are an expert in speaking the language of the Lei-ach Demons[9]; in that situation, if your group or organization needs to communicate with those demons, you will be the person with the most expert power. That does tend to give you a lot of hefty pull – I always tell people that expert power is the one base that is super beneficial and impervious to outside shocks. Take legitimate power for instance – kings and queens can be toppled in a sudden coup, while adjudicating committees can be disbanded or its members rejected for reelection. However, expertise power, a person tends to keep for the long run (unless a better expert emerges, of course). I will say this though: a person who has expert power but never demonstrates those powers will find it difficult to convince people about his or her expert power status. Take Willow or Tara or Amy for instance – all of them powerful witches in their own right; but if they didn't actually demonstrate their prowess in witchcraft, then nobody would know that they had those powers, right? The other characters in the BtVS world only knew about Willow et al.'s powers because they'd seen evidence of that. This very much applies in real life too – if you have expert power, then one should jolly well demonstrate it.

A related power to expert power is information power.[2,8] Here, one's power is dictated entirely by the fact that one has access to information that others crave and that information is only given out if the desirous recipient does what is asked of them. Some scholars consider this to be a distinct form of expert power, while others consider it as a subtype of expert power. I am personally alright with either category since there are distinct similarities and differences betwixt the two. Think of Giles again here – he can be said to possess both expert and informational power, the latter in part due to his ability to produce whatever books or information a patron may need (although skeptics could argue that Giles spends most of his time hoarding ancient artifacts and mystical manuscripts at the library and is far too busy hanging with the Scoobies, but critics will carp and cavil). I must add here that the creators of the bases of power namely John French and Bertram Raven added informational power[10] as a separate base of power in 1965 since it wasn't included in their original 1959 treatise on bases of power.

The next base of power that I will discuss is referent power.[8,10] This base has to do with how people can sometimes have the ability to assume authority without actually having any formal authority at all. Think about the trusted coworker you may have, who roughly occupies the same sort of position you have, but yet, others including you, tend to follow the direction established by that individual. Referent power is incredible because it allows individuals to assume leadership positions without actually even being appointed into those positions. The trust factor is the big factor in referent power. From the BtVS world, one person immediately comes to mind when we talk about referent power. I refer to Cordedia Chase, who was initially a bully, a popular girl yes, but quite a resolute bully, who bullied people she perceived as unpopular. Cordelia's popularity gave her quite a lot of referent power vis-à-vis the rest of the student body. Of course, she ended up eventually becoming a friend of the Scooby Gang (after she was saved multiple times by Buffy, starting with when the invisible Marcie Ross targeted Cordy).

MIXING AND MATCHING THE BASES

The above discussed bases of power are different sources of power that a person or a leader can have. Sometimes, you can have mixtures of the various bases – for instance, someone could have a legitimate base of power and also possess informational power. In that case, that individual would find that both bases of power tend to affect each other. So, if the legitimate source of power is wrested away (say, the person gets fired from a position of power, then that person's informational power also would be affected adversely). Likewise, with reward and coercive power – if one has the ability to reward, then that person would typically also have the ability to punish. One punishment that they already have control over is the ability to withhold rewards. Some leaders tend to go heavy when it comes to coercive power, and that can be counterproductive, because too much coercion is never going to be appreciated in this day and age. It may have been alright in a bygone era of medieval times but is definitely not something that a more enlightened era would support.

Personally speaking, I believe that expert power is one of the best bases of power that a person or leader should strive toward obtaining. If you have expertise, then it gives you a protective veneer of sorts. Think about it: if you rely on positional legitimate power, the minute that position is taken away, your power evaporates. Think about erstwhile Royal Family members, who are no longer "Royal." They immediately can feel the absolute loss of status and power, all because they lost the right to call themselves "Royal."

I've known some people who were rather big Kahunas in government due to their positions. The minute they retired, they immediately felt the loss of power. People who used to be uber obsequious were now avoiding their calls, or just not responding to emails or texts any longer. That's because those individuals' power entirely depended on their positions – take away the position, and the power evaporated like mist in the blazing Kalahari Desert. On the other hand, another individual didn't have any positional power but instead possessed referent power. True, that person too suffered from a loss of power on retirement, but in comparison to the other person, this individual still was able to reach out to individuals who worked with them, and those other people continued to be receptive to the now retired individual.

Expert power, on the other hand, is retained by an individual well toward the end. An expert in a particular domain or skill will continue to be an expert in that arena unless the arena itself radically transforms into something entirely different (perhaps, a tad bit like when Giles was transformed into a Fyarl Demon by the devious Ethan Rayne[11]). And remember, if you possess expert power in one arena, even if there's a lot of change that happens, your current expertise should suffice to let you get a head-start into developing expertise in the other related domain. Research has shown that effective leaders usually use a mix of expert power, referent power, and reward power. Coercive power, while tempting to use on a recalcitrant employee, is not an ideal way to use power. All it usually accomplishes is resistance, as the person being punished will obviously resent the coercive use of power.

Now that I've covered the major bases of power, it is time to persuade you (the reader) to take a dive into persuasion and influence, which is afterall what power is used to accomplish. Leaders use their power (combinations of various power bases or just one power base by itself) to influence or persuade their followers.

CAN I INFLUENCE YOU TO CHANGE YOUR MIND?

Alright, let's get straight to brass tacks now. The whole point of having power is to be able to influence or persuade your followers or employees. Take a simple example – if you're driving your snazzy convertible down Main street without wearing your seatbelt (as an aside: please don't do this! Quite an idiotic thing to do, and dangerous to boot!), a police officer can easily get you to stop, and then either fine you or ticket you, or choose to give you a stern warning. The police officer can do that because he or she has legitimate and positional power and can choose a coercive power type of outcome. Then the next time you go driving down the street, you'll make sure to put your seatbelt on, to avoid getting stopped or fined or ticketed or even getting the stern warning again.

Another example that illustrates how power is linked with persuasion can be based off on reward power. Let me use an example from an office – let's say you have a boss who has the ability to offer promotions and bonuses depending on your performance. If the boss determines that your performance or behavior is worthwhile of a reward, then you end up getting the reward. However, if you fail to do what you've been instructed to do so, then you will not be getting any rewards. You may not get punished, but the lack of a reward could be considered akin to punishment and that would be helpful in getting people to comply with orders or get persuaded by their leader.

Now, let's discuss some of the various influences or persuasion tactics that leaders or any individual really could try to influence others. You will find about 11 influence tactics that a lot of textbooks and authors refer to; however, in this book, I will be focusing on what can be termed as the core four (just so as to match the core four in BtVS namely Buffy, Xander, Willow, and Giles). These core four tactics are rational persuasion, consultation, inspirational appeals, and collaboration.[12–15] I will now introduce each tactic and provide some examples to illustrate those tactics.

Rational persuasion involves the use of logic and hard facts to explain why the requested task is essential or beneficial. This is something that we often see Rupert Giles employ throughout the BtVS series. Giles knows a lot and is usually very punctiliously logical. One of the early times where we first see him cast aside logic for a bit is during the Slayer test set by Quentin Travers of the Watcher's Council.[16] This leads to him getting fired as Slayer, or at least official Slayer for a while. But all his usual influence attempts revolved around rational persuasion, where he would use cold logic to influence the Scooby gang. This is usually what a leader who has expert power tends to use since it's a question of logic and hard facts, and their expertise in a certain domain usually lends itself well to using logic.

Consultation, on the other hand, involves seeking out other people's approval of an intended course of action and possibly amends or improves the plan. The person I think who used this influence tactic the most was probably Dawn, that is, Buffy's younger sister (originally the Key). This is understandable because even though Dawn was the Key, she was also embedded firmly as Buffy's baby sister in everyone's mind. So, essentially, she did not have a whole lot of positional or legitimate power, so in order to get that, she did need to get everyone to buy in to what she proposed. As one can guess, leaders, who lack expert power or referent power or legitimate power, are the ones who are most likely to use a consultative approach. And of course, leaders who want to be truly democratic leaders do as well, but generally speaking, leaders who use this influence tactic tend to do so because they lack other bases of power.

The third influence tactic is inspirational appeals. This one involves the use of emotionally arousing messages to inspire people to commit to a course of action. Xander from the Scooby Gang is the person who comes to mind when it comes to using this influence tactic. Throughout the series, in so many different ways, Xander is the person who relies on using inspirational appeals. He uses humor repeatedly throughout his interactions with the Scoobies in order to lighten the general mood and to get people motivated to commit to a joint course of action. You may recall that Giles in particular does not take too much of a shine to Xander's humor, but he still does grudgingly follow along with several of Xander's plans. This inspirational tactic can be used by leaders who are powerful and by leaders who lack power – it is universally usable, but as Xander's experiences tell us, your mileage may vary. If you deliver what you think is an inspirational message but which falls flat, then perhaps the message isn't really inspirational, and it may be time to go back to the drawing board.

The final influence tactic I'll discuss here (remember, we're just focusing on the core four) is collaboration. Here, the influencer offers help or assistance with completing tasks. This tactic is somewhat linked with consultation, but the difference here is that the leader does need to be specific while assigning tasks or taking on tasks. Both Willow and Tara (to a lesser extent) used this particular influence tactic while discussing options and plans. In essence, here the leader influences his or her follower by demonstrating to them that they too are invested in the plan and are, indeed, collaborating together to show their dedication.

So, these were the core four influence tactics, but as I mentioned, there are other influence tactics you can read about (such as ingratiation, legitimation, etc.). I'm not going to be discussing those here, but they do make for interesting reading. However, as I mentioned earlier, these core four or combinations of the core four influence tactics usually suffice for leaders to be able to influence or persuade others. But the overall lesson here to understand is that in order to influence, you must have power. And in order to get power, you must be able to influence. It's rather an interesting dilemma if you happen to be weak in either area, then the other area suffers too. Well, I also just realized that Anya never does make it in this chapter – but I do guarantee she'll feature in plenty others.

SUMMARY

This chapter presents information about the various bases of power and provides examples from BtVS that illustrate these bases of power. Additionally, I also discuss the core influence and persuasion tactics that leaders can use, and there too provide some examples from the Buffyverse to illustrate those tactics. In the next chapter, I will take on the somber responsibility of discussing responsibility and what it means for a leader (to walk a Slayer's path, or at least, a righteous Slayer's path).

REFERENCES

1. French, J. R., & Raven, B. (1959). The bases of social power. *Studies in Social Power, 150*, 167–177.

2. Northouse, P. G. (2025). *Leadership: Theory and practice*. Sage Publications.

3. Kudisch, J. D., Poteet, M. L., Dobbins, G. H., Rush, M. C., & Russell, J. E. (1995). Expert power, referent power, and charisma: Toward the resolution of a theoretical debate. *Journal of Business and Psychology, 10*, 177–195.

4. Greenleaf, R. K. (2013). *Servant leadership: A journey into the nature of legitimate power and greatness*. Paulist Press.

5. Cheng, Y. N., Hu, C., Wang, S., & Huang, J. C. (2024). Political context matters: A joint effect of coercive power and perceived organizational politics on abusive supervision and silence. *Asia Pacific Journal of Management, 41*(1), 81–106.

6. Körner, R., Overbeck, J. R., Körner, E., & Schütz, A. (2022). How the linguistic styles of Donald Trump and Joe Biden reflect different forms of power. *Journal of Language and Social Psychology, 41*(6), 631–658.

7. Hollander, E. P. (1993). Legitimacy, power, and influence: A perspective on relational features of leadership. In M. M. Chemers & R. Ayman (Eds.), *Leadership theory and research: Perspectives and directions* (pp. 29–47). Academic Press.

8. Humphrey, R. H. (2013). *Effective leadership: Theory, cases, and applications*. Sage Publications.

9. Fandom. (n.d.). *Lei-ach demon*. Buffy the Vampire Slayer Wiki. Retrieved January 24, 2024, from https://buffy.fandom.com/wiki/Lei-ach_demon

10. Raven, B. H. (1993). The bases of power: Origins and recent developments. *Journal of Social Issues, 49*(4), 227–251.

11. Whedon, J. (Writer & Director). (2000). A new man (Season 4, Episode 12) [TV episode]. In *Buffy the Vampire Slayer*. Mutant Enemy Productions.

12. Charbonneau, D. (2004). Influence tactics and perceptions of transformational leadership. *Leadership & Organization Development Journal, 25*(7), 565–576.

13. Falbe, C. M., & Yukl, G. (1992). Consequences for managers of using single influence tactics and combinations of tactics. *Academy of Management Journal, 35*(3), 638–652.

14. Yukl, G., & Tracey, J. B. (1992). Consequences of influence tactics used with subordinates, peers, and the boss. *Journal of Applied Psychology, 77*(4), 525.

15. Mayfield, C. O., & O'Donnell, M. (2025). Proactive influence tactics that increase work engagement for remote employees. *Management Research Review, 48*(3), 383–400.

16. Fury, D. (Writer), & Gershman, M. (Director). (1999). Helpless (Season 3, Episode 12) [TV episode]. In *Buffy the Vampire Slayer*. Mutant Enemy Productions.

3

RESPONSIBILITY – LEADERS MUST WALK A SLAYER'S PATH

One concept which usually tags along when one is discussing leadership is the big R word, namely, Responsibility. Leaders have so much responsibility thrust upon their shoulders, be it responsibility for the organization or unit or country they lead. And of course, one should also remember that leaders are responsible for the people that they lead – there are multiple flavors and types of responsibilities that leaders have to be mindful about, and in this chapter, I'll discuss some of those responsibilities and offer up some examples from BtVS. In particular, I think this chapter will be rather Slayer heavy, in terms of examples and situation citing. After all, let's face it, in the BtVS world, the focal leader is pretty much the Slayer. She (I'm referring to all Slayers not just Buffy) may follow directions and be led by others in several arenas, but in the end, the Slayer is the focal leader in this particular world context. Why, even Andrew Wells from the Trio recognized Buffy as the undisputable focal leader of the Scooby Gang, much to Xander's chagrin.

In this chapter, I will start off by discussing the concept of responsibility and delineate the various ways by which we can start to think about leaders and responsibility. Then, I will discuss some of the pros and cons of responsible leadership. I will also illustrate with several examples and situations from BtVS in order to help us understand leadership responsibility and learn to be truly responsible leaders ourselves. Let's get on with the program and dive straight into what responsibility entails.

(HARD R)RESPONSIBILITY

I suppose we should first define the word itself. This is one of those words that usually gets defined with a circular definition or by defining it as the opposite of its antonym (so, one could say that responsibility is the absence of irresponsibility, at which point lexicographers will probably all rise up in rebellion at this casual shredding of definitions). Responsibility can be thought of as being synonymous with duty, be it fiduciary or otherwise. The duty to do right by others, and to do right by your group or organization.[1-4] Scholars have argued that responsibility in leadership is not just tied to accountability or dependability, but instead multifaceted, wherein the responsible leader needs to consider multiple stakeholders (based off on stakeholder theory[5]). And an integral part of responsibility is the concept of appropriateness, or the ability to act in appropriate fashion to a situation or event.[6-8] Of course, it is also vital for a responsible leader to be able to be so – if one lacks the ability or capacity to act or respond, then of course, the entire question is moot.

From BtVS, one can easily see how Buffy fits into the role of responsible leader, as not only is she fully capable of fighting the various vampires, demons, and demonic entities around, but she shows an incredible sense of responsibility throughout the entire series. Think about when the Master was the big baddie during season 1, where it was prophesized that he would kill the Slayer. In the beginning, Buffy is scared and fearful (do remember that she's only 16 years old at this point), and even temporarily quits being Slayer.[9] But then tragedy (involving vampires and their brutal killing of the audiovisual club students) strikes, Buffy realizes that it is her duty to embrace her destiny even though her destiny appears to be dark and forbidding. She even comes back to prevent Giles from standing in on her stead. She does the responsible action and takes on the Master even though she believes she would die in the process, which she kinda does, but Xander resuscitates her[9] (which turns out to be a good thing else the BtVS series would just be a season long). Buffy does that for the greater good, and she's willing to sacrifice herself for others (which is something all good Slayers have to be willing to do).

Another situation which shows how Buffy takes on responsibility for others circumstances happens during the season finale of the fifth season.[10] This is when the Hell-goddess Glory is about to break down the barriers between the dimensions and that could convert Earth into a literal Hell. In the process, a portal opens up, which unleashes all sorts of hellish creatures which emerge from within it. The portal would not close until Dawn was completely exsanguinated, thanks to the devious Doc (another Demon who was secretly a worshipper of Glorificus) having cut her. Dawn too is willing to sacrifice herself to close the portal, but Buffy stops her and consoles her, and then sacrifices herself to the portal to make it close.

Yet another scenario which highlights how Buffy takes on responsibility was when her mother Joyce unexpectedly dies,[11] and all the responsibility of the home and finances, and taking care of Dawn, etc., fall upon Buffy's shoulders. While this situation may not seem as significant as some of the other BtVS goddess fighting or vampire fighting situations, I would argue that it is perhaps more significant than the others. This situation, that is, the loss of a parental figure, can be incredibly stressful to rebound from for any person, be it a Slayer or a non-Slayer. And Buffy has to shoulder a lot of the responsibility after Joyce's death – while, it does bring her and Dawn closer together, the fact of the matter is that caring for Dawn (and Joyce, when she was ill) involves Buffy having to drop out of college, and take up employment in the Doublemeat Palace[12] (a decidedly unexciting prospect, but one nevertheless that helps pay the Summers sisters bills).

While obviously, most leaders will not typically be in such life or death situations (unless they're in law enforcement or the military) involving having to literally sacrifice themselves; there are other kinds of sacrifices, which leaders have to often make. This could mean sacrificing their work–life balance, or their vacation time, or even their daily sleep. The sacrifice could also entail a financial one; during financially strapped times, it may be necessary for the leader to sacrifice their own salaries or bonuses in order to keep the company afloat or to avoid firing any of the employees. Think about what the Nintendo CEO Satoru (not Gojo) Iwata did when the company was struggling financially. He cut his own salary by half[13] in order to avoid laying off any employees. Now that is sacrifice which seems majorly unlikely in today's climate – one can hardly imagine any of the Techbro CEOs of present time to showcase sacrifice. They would rather just fire or layoff thousands of employees instead of sacrificing anything themselves. More like a wayward Faith than a sincere Buffy, really.

When one looks at or reads about some of the irresponsible leaders around us on our planet (and other Hell-dimensions, one may add), it makes us question the veracity of the eudemonic assumption (that by the way just refers to the assumption that people have a natural inclination toward moral goodness and is not just an old-world alternative spelling of a European Demon). But then when you see truly responsible leaders showcasing responsibility, then it does restore your faith in the eudemonic assumption, a fair bit. However, sadly, there are enough cases of irresponsibility that overshadow any cases of responsibility.[14-16] Corruption, scams, and unmitigated greed are often tied in with irresponsibility, and it does feel like overall leader virtuousness is dying. But then you do need to consider that responsible leadership comes imbued with virtue.[14] So, if you find a responsible leader acting with keen responsibility, then you know that individual is a virtuous soul (an Angel instead of an Angelus, so to speak).

Now let's discuss some of the advantages and beneficial consequences of being a responsible leader. And I suppose, some discussion should also be catered toward the pitfalls of responsible leadership.

MANY PROS AND SOME CONS

There are a host of benefits that arise from responsible or virtuous leadership. The biggest benefit of course is the fact that followers tend to be incredibly loyal when they work with responsible leaders. Turnover intention or desire to leave among such employees is rather minimal and that can be beneficial for organizations. Think about Buffy here – even though the rest of the Scooby Gang get irritated with her at times due to her steadfast sense of responsibility, they would never dream of abandoning her. Discerning leaders will point out here that sometimes that did happen (e.g., when Willow turned into Dark Willow,[17] or when Anya returned to her roots as an evil Vengeance Demon[18]), but that can be explained by the simple narrative that loyalty does not mean unstinted and sheep-like loyalty throughout every single situation. Disagreements happen at times, but when it matters, loyal followers come back and do not depart. Xander is perhaps the best example of that sort of loyalty spirit, no matter how upset he may be, he never truly abandons the Scooby Gang (although, I guess he does do that to Anya). I must point out here that I am still a bit miffed with Joss Whedon for having Xander abandon Anya on their wedding day[19] – totally out of character, I still feel that it would have been so much better to have continued with the XAnya ship.

Crashing it on rocks did nothing for anybody, but I digress. Let's head back to the discussion on responsible leadership consequences.

Another big advantage of responsible leaders is that they can get their organizations and their people to start being socially responsible too. Think about it, anytime you see a company or organization engaging in social responsibility, you can directly credit a leader for that. Sure, there is corporate greenwashing where leaders cynically pretend like their companies are socially responsible, whereas the reality is that they're just doing that to enhance their reputations. But when you have genuine cases of social responsibility, you can guarantee that the leader in charge or one of the leader's direct followers is behind the movement toward social responsibility. Think about Indra Nooyi, the former CEO of Pepsi Co: she was the reason behind Pepsi's getting involved with health foods.[20] Without her, it is doubtful that the company would have even stepped into the health food domain. Responsible leaders are instrumental in helping their organizations become more socially responsible. Consider the example of Buffy when she ends up being close to Riley and the Initiative and discovers that they've been doing experiments on all sorts of demons, regardless of whether they're harmful or not. Buffy ends up exposing their unethical experiments,[21] which indirectly leads to the diminishing of the Initiative. She does after all strive to be responsible for the safety of all innocent beings, regardless of whether they're demons or werewolves or humans.

While responsible leadership has its virtues, there are definitely some unintended and possibly detrimental consequences arising from exercising (what you think is) responsible leadership. The biggest issue is when a leader believes that he or she is being responsible, but in reality, that thought is mere delusion. Think about the leaders who operated during genocidal regimes and who took decisions that we today recognize as being awful. They probably thought they were doing the responsible thing and would be affronted by any criticism being cast at their decision-making process. Similarly, in today's business world, think about the leaders who close and shut down locations even if those locations are profitable. The recent Red Lobster almost-bankruptcy crisis[22] was fueled entirely by vulture capitalists, who decided to swoop in and shut down locations even though there wasn't a clear profitability issue. Something similar happened with the case of Toys-R-Us,[23] which did go bankrupt thanks to the actions of vulture capitalist investors (who one can add were entirely convinced that they were acting responsibly). A direct example from BtVS that fits into this paradigm is the Watchers Council headed by Quentin Travers. This council always acted in frustratingly oblique ways, by arguing that they were adhering to tradition. Some of their actions could easily be interpreted as being detrimental to the safety of Slayers personally, as well as to the overall mission entrusted to the Slayers. How can a Slayer be truly effective if she is being burdened by an officious and rigid bureaucracy, which is more obstructionist than helpful? The Watchers Council would probably argue that they were being responsible and sticking to the goals of their organization. However, as later events unfolded, with Caleb and the First Evil in the seventh season, the Watchers Council gets bombed out of existence[24] just when they finally decide to start being helpful to Buffy. Otherwise, throughout the series, they are portrayed as being useless and ineffectual, and as I mentioned, rather obstructionist. But lest anyone have any doubt, rest assured that nobody on the Watchers Council (barring Giles or Wesley Wyndham-Pryce) ever thought they were doing anything irresponsible – they really did fancy themselves as the purveyors of responsibility.

Another organization and its leaders (who thought themselves the concierge of responsibility) from BtVS is the Initiative. This was a secret organization which was headed by Maggie Walsh and included Riley Finn in it. Again, the organization was supposedly created to engage in acts of responsibility, chiefly to keep people safe by studying and researching demons and vampires. But unbeknownst to many, the Initiative and Maggie Walsh were not exactly acting in responsible or virtuous ways. For starters, they were not averse to carrying out brutal experiments on anyone they perceived as less than human. So, Spike, our favorite Billy Idol resembling Vampire, had a pain chip inserted into his brain, which prevented him from getting blood, and he ended up having to go to the Scooby Gang to beg for sustenance. Now that may not seem like too brutal an experiment, as after all, at the time when the pain chip was put in, Spike was a rather evil being.

However, the initiative also treated Oz (Willow's ex-boyfriend, and a Werewolf during full moon nights) rather brutally, just because of his Werewolf tendencies, which by the way, he only became due to having been bitten by his cousin Jordy. If the Initiative were truly led by a responsible leader, then that fact would have been considered in evaluating whether or not to even capture Oz in the first place. And additionally, if Maggie Walsh were truly a responsible leader, she would not have sanctioned Project 314 or the creation of the biomechanical demonoid Adam, who ended up causing a lot of damage throughout Sunnydale. Ironically, this very same Adam was also responsible for killing Maggie Walsh.[25] Alas, but an ounce of true responsibility would have perhaps prevented those tragic circumstances. Even though Adam was polite and all, he still killed Maggie Walsh, impaling her with a Polgara bone-skewer, which Maggie had gotten transplanted in Adam. Maggie was not being a responsible leader (even though she was convinced that she was), as she was acting in ways that proved to be dangerous, and acting without any shred of humanity. Ruthlessness is not a good ingredient in responsible leadership, especially because Maggie was doing everything she could to control all of the Initiative members, including Riley (who she had gotten a behavior modifier chip implanted into). So, to reiterate, just because a leader thinks he or she is being a responsible leader does not make them into a responsible leader. They have to emphasize responsibility to multiple stakeholders and truly be aware that they're not becoming ineffective or destructive leaders all in the name of responsibility. The next section will discuss how a person can act or behave like a responsible leader.

HOW DOES A PERSON ACT LIKE A RESPONSIBLE LEADER?

Well, for starters – the biggest difference between a responsible leader and one who skates on irresponsibly is that the former category of leader takes on his or her duty seriously, and with a core of moral conscience behind them. Consider Buffy and compare her with Faith – both were equally powerful, but Buffy had a moral conscience, which Faith lacked. That alone ruled out Faith from becoming a responsible leader, not to mention her getting corrupted by Mayor Wilkins in the third season. As I mentioned previously, Buffy tried her best to protect everyone, not just humans. She protected anyone who needed protection and was an innocent party or bystander. Faith had no such compunctions and was content to do whatever it took to accomplish her goals (be they as twisted as possible). I suppose that's why the series was called Buffy the Vampire Slayer and not Faith the Vampire Slayer (hmm.... In a battle between FtVS vs BtVS, the latter still has a better ring to it).

So basically, the first step to take to be a truly responsible leader is to evaluate if you are incorporating virtue and goodness in your decision making. Do your decisions harm anyone innocent, directly or indirectly? If they do, then you're not engaging in responsible leadership. When in doubt, look at the harm factor. If you are intentionally causing harm to others despite being cautioned by others, then your leadership is not truly responsible leadership. If you're unintentionally causing harm, and then find out, and subsequently effect changes to eliminate the harm, then that's a step back into being a responsible leader.

Another step to take to be a responsible leader is to adopt a long-term perspective on decision making. Don't think of short-term gains or benefits – looking at improving quarterly performances when the end result could be disastrous for your company is something a lot of irresponsible leaders do. Faith's aligning with the Mayor was a perfect example of short-term decision making – while she probably thought she was seeking out a bright future for herself, she should have realized that it would have been very short term, indeed, for herself as well as for Sunnydale. Once the Mayor got what he wanted, that is, became a powerful demon, there would have been no guarantee that he would have kept his word to Faith. Absolute power breeds corruption, and Mayor Wilkins was already quite corrupt, and Faith knew that, but she still allowed her dark side to come to the forefront and betray her real allies in the process.

This is similar to the leaders who take on destructive short-term focused decisions, without sparing a thought for what the future could mean. Just consider the leaders who lay off their employees en masse to make their books look good. But it's all an irresponsible façade and not really indicative of a clean bill of health. Similar to a person sucking in their stomach to appear like they don't have a paunch. Adopting a long-term perspective in making decisions is another key step for people to take in order to be responsible leaders. Wholly operating with a short-term focus in mind is a sureshot way of becoming an irresponsible leader since whatever value you do generate is only going to be ephemeral and will vanish like dewdrops under a blazing sun (not unlike how vampires similarly vanish into a pile of dust in the presence of sunlight).

The third way to become a responsible leader is to avoid taking on a laisse-faire approach to leadership – you know, the kind of leadership which is characterized by a complete lack of leadership.[26] The leader might as well not be present for all the non-leadership they provide in the case of laisse-faire leaders. Look at how Buffy usually patrols the town diligently, even when she's not feeling like it, or is feeling low. Well yes, granted, that she did run away from Sunnydale but that did happen after the extremely trau-matic event of Buffy having to stab Angel (she was battling the evil soulless Angelus who suddenly turned into Angel) to prevent Acathla from trigger-ing and setting off an apocalypse. So, it is a bit understandable that Buffy ran away because the heartache was too much to bear. A laisse-faire leader would probably never suffer any such existential heartache simply because that person would not even have the slightest clue about any consequences of their non-action. So, to sum it up, don't be a laisse-faire or lazy-faire (as it could be renamed as) leader, but instead take charge, and *patrol* your organi-zation or country, keeping an eye out for any risks or threats.

SUMMARY

This chapter presents information about responsible leadership and how exactly BtVS examples (especially centered on how the Slayer must embrace a wholistic responsibility for the protection of all innocents) illustrate what responsible and irresponsible leadership are. I also discuss the pros and cons of responsible leadership, especially the ones that emerge when one believes they're being responsible, but they're really not. I finally discuss how some-one can be a responsible leader and avoid being an irresponsible leader. In the next chapter, we will put on a tweed jacket, and maybe brew up a pot of tea, since we're going to be diving into the topic of mentorship, and Giles (and perhaps Wesley for a bit) will feature prominently in the third chapter.

REFERENCES

1. Siegel, D. S. (2014). Responsible leadership. *Academy of Management Perspectives*, *28*(3), 221–223.

2. Waldman, D. A., & Balven, R. M. (2014). Responsible leadership: Theoretical issues and research directions. *Academy of Management Perspectives*, *28*(3), 224–234.

3. Stone-Johnson, C. (2014). Responsible leadership. *Educational Administration Quarterly*, *50*(4), 645–674.

4. Starratt, R. J. (2005). Responsible leadership. *The Educational Forum*, *69*(2), 124–133. https://doi.org/10.1080/00131720508984676.

5. Maak, T., & Pless, N. M. (2006). Responsible leadership in a stakeholder society – A relational perspective. *Journal of Business Ethics, 66*, 99–115.

6. Waldman, D. A., & Galvin, B. M. (2008). Alternative perspectives of responsible leadership. *Organizational Dynamics, 37*(4), 327–341.

7. Miska, C., & Mendenhall, M. E. (2018). Responsible leadership: A mapping of extant research and future directions. *Journal of Business Ethics, 148*, 117–134.

8. Pearce, C. L., Wassenaar, C. L., & Manz, C. C. (2014). Is shared leadership the key to responsible leadership? *Academy of Management Perspectives, 28*(3), 275–288.

9. Whedon, J. (Writer & Director). (1997). Prophecy girl (Season 1, Episode 12) [TV episode]. In *Buffy the Vampire Slayer*. Mutant Enemy Productions.

10. Whedon, J. (Writer & Director). (2001). The gift (Season 5, Episode 22) [TV episode]. In *Buffy the Vampire Slayer*. Mutant Enemy Productions.

11. Whedon, J. (Writer & Director). (2001). The body (Season 5, Episode 16) [TV episode]. In *Buffy the Vampire Slayer*. Mutant Enemy Productions.

12. Espenson, J. (Writer), & Marck, N. (Director). (2002). Doublemeat palace (Season 6, Episode 12) [TV episode]. In *Buffy the Vampire Slayer*. Mutant Enemy Productions.

13. Jackson, S. (2024, February 13). *Nintendo CEO once halved his salary to prevent layoffs, and it worked – Why that's so uncommon today.* CNBC. https://www.cnbc.com/2024/02/13/nintendo-ceo-once-halved-salary-to-prevent-layoffs-why-thats-uncommon.html

14. Cameron, K. (2011). Responsible leadership as virtuous leadership. *Journal of Business Ethics, 98*(1), 25–35.

15. Boddy, C. R. (2013). Corporate psychopaths: Uncaring citizens, irresponsible leaders. *Journal of Corporate Citizenship, 49*, 8–16.

16. Oplatka, I. (2016). "Irresponsible leadership" and unethical practices in schools: Conceptual framework of the 'dark side' of educational leadership. In A. Normore & J. Brooks (Eds.), *The dark side of leadership: Identifying and overcoming unethical practice in organizations* (pp. 1–18). Emerald Group Publishing.

17. Noxon, M. (Writer), & Solomon, D. (Director). (2002). Villains (Season 6, Episode 20) [TV episode]. In *Buffy the Vampire Slayer*. Mutant Enemy Productions.

18. Goddard, D. (Writer), & Solomon, D. (Director). (2002). Selfless (Season 7, Episode 5) [TV episode]. In *Buffy the Vampire Slayer*. Mutant Enemy Productions.

19. Kirschner, R. (Writer), & Solomon, D. (Director). (2002). Hell's bells (Season 6, Episode 16) [TV episode]. In *Buffy the Vampire Slayer*. Mutant Enemy Productions.

20. Nooyi, I. K., & Govindarajan, V. (2020). Becoming a better corporate citizen. *Harvard Business Review, 98*(2), 94–103.

21. Petrie, D. (Writer), & Contner, J. A. (Director). (1999). The initiative (Season 4, Episode 7) [TV episode]. In *Buffy the Vampire Slayer*. Mutant Enemy Productions.

22. Morgenson, G. (2024, February 23). *Private equity rolled Red Lobster – And it's not the only one*. NBC News. https://www.nbcnews.com/business/consumer/private-equity-rolled-red-lobster-rcna153397

23. Morgan, J., & Nasir, M. A. (2021). Financialised private equity finance and the debt gamble: The case of Toys R Us. *New Political Economy*, 26(3), 455–471.

24. Goddard, D. (Writer), & Solomon, D. (Director). (2002). Never leave me (Season 7, Episode 9) [TV episode]. In *Buffy the Vampire Slayer*. Mutant Enemy Productions.

25. Fury, D. (Writer), & Contner, J. A. (Director). (2000). The I in Team (Season 4, Episode 5) [TV episode]. In *Buffy the Vampire Slayer*. Mutant Enemy Productions.

26. Skogstad, A., Einarsen, S., Torsheim, T., Aasland, M. S., & Hetland, H. (2007). The destructiveness of laissez-faire leadership behavior. *Journal of Occupational Health Psychology*, 12(1), 80–92. https://doi.org/10.1037/1076-8998.12.1.80

4

EFFECTIVE MENTORSHIP – A GILESIAN (AND OTHERS) APPROACH

I have always held firm my belief that one of the best things a leader can have access to in their lives is a mentor. A good mentor can open doors for you, and can show you the way, and, indeed, help inculcate skills in you that can be transformational for your life. I have had several excellent mentors in my own life, so many folks who've impacted my own leadership philosophy and approach to decision-making and life. I have also crossed paths with a mentor who pretty much dropped me within a few interactions inexplicably at that. He must have gotten grumpy for some odd reason, well, I guess his hart… I mean heart wasn't in it, but in any case, he wasn't my dean, so it was fine, I suppose. Better to not mentor someone when you're not interested, and in the process, ruin the prospects of that individual finding a better mentor.

Anyway, passing along from that unpleasant sojourn into my memory lanes, let's get to the topic at hand, namely, Mentorship. The Buffy verse offers so many great examples that illustrate good mentorship, and poor mentorship as well (one must add). The reason I named this chapter after Giles though is quite simple – as Buffy's first Watcher, Rupert Giles is the primary mentor in Buffy's life, especially after she became a Slayer. His qualities had an indelible effect on Buffy's own philosophy and Slayer'esque style. Without Giles' moral compass guiding her, it stands to reason that she could have well become similar to how Faith initially turned out. Imagine if Giles had been as twisted as Mayor Wilkins or as ineffectual as Wesley was in the beginning; Buffy may have turned out completely different; in one case, she could have been an Evil Slayer, or in the other case, she could have been a completely misguided one. Now granted that she had a strong moral compass of her own, but Giles' values certainly rubbed off on her and impacted her own value system.

In this chapter, I will begin by discussing the importance of mentorship in a leadership context and follow that with a discussion of how a leader can be involved in the entire process of mentorship. One can be a mentee, but one can also be a mentor – and being involved in both capacities can be incredibly useful and beneficial. I will illustrate all of this with various examples and incidents from BtVS as the motif of the book does lend itself to that. Next, I will discuss how we can get more people involved in mentorship and in a useful and effective way. I will also discuss how a mentor can be a sponsor, and why it is important for mentees to seek out sponsors as opposed to passive mentors. So, let's saunter over to learning more about mentors, and their importance.

THE IMPORTANCE OF BEING EARNEST IN MENTORSHIP

As I mentioned earlier, I consider mentorship to be supremely important in helping people improve their skills and their professional networks. In many ways, a mentor can help you break barriers, which you may have never realized existed, prior to the mentor's telling you about it. Take Buffy for instance – she knew little to nothing about Slayer history or about the demons and vampires, and various orders about. Giles was instrumental in helping expand Buffy's knowledge and prowess as a Slayer. While he may have been a rebellious Ripper[1] in his days of youth, by the time he comes into Buffy's life as a Watcher, Giles is the quintessential intellectual librarian and perfectly adept at filling the empty father figure spot in Buffy's life (thanks to her perennially absent biological father Hank Summers).

Effective leaders typically tend to have good mentors,[2-5] well okay, there are many self-reliant leaders who never had mentors, etc., but for the most part, effective leaders do tend to have good mentors. Someone who helped them early on, perhaps in ways that they did not immediately recognize. Think about it – someone who becomes a President or a CEO of a company did not simply get put into that position without having people mold them into the leader they eventually become. Yes, granted again that there are times when a person is thrust onto the throne, without having a formal mentor guide them, but there would have been many informal mentors along the way. Mentors do not have to be formally assigned or chosen[6-8]; there are lots of examples of informal mentors being highly instrumental in people's careers. In my own career (apart from the one formal mentor who called our mentor–mentee relationship quits and was decidedly not a good mentor for me), all of the other good mentors I've had have been informal mentors.

These mentors be they informal or formal are able to relay their experiences and knowledge to their mentees in ways by which the mentee actually understands and is able to use that knowledge themselves. Let's take the case of Wesley Wyndham-Pryce for a bit now – he was decidedly inferior to the much superior Watcher, Giles. In fact, the only reason Wesley even appears[9] in the first place is due to the machinations of the Watcher's Council, who wanted a more pliant Watcher as opposed to the harder to control Giles. This, of course, then led to Wesley becoming Faith's Watcher even though that didn't take too long to fray and falter. Actually, come to think of it, we could probably think of mentors even in the vampire world or the demon world. From the vampire world, one could easily cast Angel or Angelus as he was initially in the role of a mentor. The initially nascent vampire Spike for instance probably only became as vicious and successful as he did, thanks to Angelus, who mentored him in the fine dark vampiric arts of slaughtering people. True, the mentoring wasn't provided out of any sense of responsibility, but it was given, and without it, Spike would probably not have survived too long, and never gotten to be part of what Darla (in the related show *Angel*) called the Whirlwind (i.e., Angelus, Darla, Drusilla, and finally Spike) who caused a wave of destruction and dead throughout the 18th and 19th centuries. While none of this mentoring could be said to be kind or nurturing – truth be told, rather a twisted bunch of mentors in the Whirlwind, with them having sired each other, as in Darla sired Angelus, and Angelus sired Drusilla, and Drusilla sired Spike. But on the whole, the mentoring seemed to work since each vampire in this motley crew did turn out to be incredibly successful vampires (as in being highly dangerous and feared across continents).

Another example of mentoring can be seen in a demonic context, when one considers D'Hoffryn, the head of the vengeance demons. He was the one who reached out to Aud (Anya's previous human name, in Sweden in the year 860), after her incredible act of vengeance against her lover at the time Olaf. D'Hoffryn reached out to Aud[10] and dangled the carrot of making her into a vengeance demon, which she agreed to. And then as Anyanka the vengeance demon, she pretty much turned out to be one of D'Hoffryn's favorite proteges, much to the envy of Halfrek (another vengeance demon, who was initially a rival but then turned out to be Anyanka's best friend). But this mentoring by D'Hoffryn was incredibly useful, as Anyanka grew into being one of the most successful vengeance demons – no wonder, she was one of the favorites of D'Hoffryn. I would argue that D'Hoffryn's mentorship was quite possibly kinder and a more encouraging way to mentor, especially when compared to the mentoring going on in the Whirlwind (i.e., the Darla and Angelus clan).

Of course, D'Hoffryn's kindness doesn't last permanently – when Anya spurns him in season seven, he seems mightily ticked off and even sends assassins to kill her.[11,12] One would remember that that's one of the reasons why a suddenly powerless Anya rejoins the Scooby Gang to avail of the protection that Buffy and the rest could provide her with. This was doubly so due to the First Evil, which was hellbent on destroying the entire line of Slayers, including all the potential Slayers out there in the world. But circling back to mentorship, sometimes when mentorship turns bad, there can certainly be adverse consequences of it. But let's spring along to learning how one can get involved in the mentorship process.

HOW TO BE INVOLVED IN THE MENTORSHIP PROCESS

The primary way for a person to be involved in mentorship is to first want to be involved in the process. Now, I realize that may sound a trifle bit facetious, but it bears saying. One cannot simply drag a Greyhound to a race, if the hound has no desire to run; similarly, one cannot be involved in the mentorship process if one lacks any desire to be involved. Now that I have that out of the way, let's get into core details. Circling back to my previous statement, one really does need to want to be involved in mentoring. There are no gains to be gotten if one is getting into mentoring in a half-hearted or lackadaisical fashion. If you're signing up to be a mentor to someone, you had jolly well (as Wesley Wyndham-Pryce would perhaps put it) be truly committed to the task. One should not simply sign up to be a mentor unless one wants to truly make a difference in the mentee's life.

Vice versa, one shouldn't seek out a mentor unless one is committed to being a thoughtful and diligent mentee. Why waste someone's time, right? There were certainly times in the Buffy series, where you could see Giles struggling a bit with the idea of being a mentor because he perceived that Buffy wasn't being serious enough. But of course, being Giles, he never stopped caring for her, even when he had to actually defy the Watcher's Council. So, now that we've established the needing to want to be involved and needing to be committed and serious about it, let's get down to brass tacks.

After ensuring that you truly do want to be a mentor, it's now time to reach out and get in touch with organizations or groups that are involved in mentoring. For instance, if you happen to be working in an organization, seek out a mentoring group or unit[13–15] within your organization, to have them perhaps help you in pairing with a suitable mentee. This is usually manageable because many organizations have formal mechanisms for encouraging their employees to be engaged in mentoring. This sort of step can be incredibly fulfilling from a professional or career perspective. However, there are certainly plenty of times when one's organization does not have any formal way to encourage the mentoring process. What does a would-be-mentor do at that point? Well, as cliché as it may sound to say, in those times you basically need to grab the Minotaur by its horns, or the Chaos Demon by its antlers, and wrestle it to the ground (although in fairness, the BtVS series does not feature a Minotaur like creature at all. Pity, it would have been fun to have seen Giles have an annoyed repartee with either Spike or Xander about the Minotaur).

Basically, if your organization lacks a formal mechanism or process to handle mentoring, you just have to create that in an informal way. Be available and accessible to juniors in your organization and be visible. If you're visible across various levels in your company and give off an impression of being approachable, then you'll find it easy to attract potential mentees to you. I've personally found that informal processes work great while seeking out mentors or mentees. So, if a formal mechanism doesn't exist, you can circumvent that by using an informal process, to get involved in mentorship. But do be aware that formal or informal, it is necessary to be absolutely sincere in wanting to be involved in mentorship. Half-hearted or insincere efforts are plainly useless, and about as futile and embarrassing as Andrew Wells' efforts to bond with the various potential Slayers and Dawn.

GO THE EXTRA MILE AS A MENTOR – BE A SPONSOR

Off late, I've been reading a lot of information about how mentors ought to be doing more than just passive mentoring. The right approach as per several thought-leaders (most particularly Ann Hewlett[16]) is that mentors ought to be doing a bit of sponsoring as opposed to just being passive mentors. This to me makes a lot of sense – in essence (not attempting a rhyme here, it just happened), sponsoring your mentee means helping your mentee gain power. The world's leading expert on power, Jeffrey Pfeffer,[17–19] has often remarked and spoken that good leadership developers are the ones who help their proteges gain power. That is exactly what sponsorship implies. You don't simply show a path, but you actually get your mentee to traverse the path.

Now, as twisted as it may sound, from my perspective, Mayor Wilkins was the one character from BtVS who truly exemplified this actively sponsor and not just passively mentor philosophy to the hilt. Yes, granted, he was an evil individual, and his goals would not quite lead to a universal utopia, but as a mentor for Faith, he was perhaps more archetypical of a sponsor than a passive mentor. He wasn't content to just let her be his mentee, but he actively sponsored her to attain more power herself. He also actively works to get her and keep her out of legal trouble. Recall that Faith murdered the deputy mayor Allan Finch,[20] and instead of being appalled at that, Mayor Wilkins actively protected Faith. If that isn't sponsoring a mentee, what else is? Sponsors protect and help their mentees; of course, I'm not suggesting that sponsors help their mentees commit crimes and get away from it, but the protection aspect of being a sponsor is integral to being one.

Another integral aspect of being a sponsor is that there has to be power available in the sponsor. Think about someone being mentored by a person who has minimal power – what real use is that for the mentee? To be a sponsor, the mentor has to actually have a voice at the table. Consider an example from the BtVS world, Clement, the loose-skinned demon.[21] He was perhaps one of the most innocuous characters from the entire series and extremely likeable. However, one would be hard-pressed to consider him as powerful. Clement would make for a great babysitter, and he did do that, when Buffy asked him to "babysit" Dawn during the time when Willow had become Dark Willow. But he would not be a great sponsor since he really didn't have a whole lot of power. So, power is definitely something that a sponsor has got to possess because you cannot transfer or impart something to others that you yourself lack.

Only if an individual has power, will that person be accorded a voice at the table. And without a voice at the table, a mentor, no matter how willing he or she is, will be unable to transcend and become a sponsor. And it does seem in today's hypercompetitive world, that people need sponsors. You need someone to advocate for you in order for you to grow, and this goes for leaders as well. You might be the one with the potential to be a great leader, but if nobody with existing power and voice advocates for you, that potential will be snuffed out. It'll be similar to all the potential Slayers who didn't go on to become actual Slayers themselves. In the BtVS world, Caleb in his serving of the First Evil, ended up killing several potential Slayers, and also killed off most of the Watchers in the Watchers Council. That way he ensured that none of the potential Slayers would go on to become future Slayers – what better way to do that than to eliminate any possible sponsors.

And then one more integral aspect of being a sponsor is to give your mentees enough cover so as to be able to take risks. In other words, a sponsor provides a safety net of sorts to ensure that the mentee doesn't go tumbling into a bottomless crevice. Only by taking risks, can a person really start to get positive gains, and a sponsor can help his or her mentee take risks, by being there to help them if they stumble. One does not wish to replicate a scene that would be reminiscent of the time when Angel/Angelus was pulled into hell.[22] A sponsor with power and voice at the table is exactly what is needed.

The above few paragraphs discuss what attributes a sponsor or an active mentor needs to possess, and a person intending to be a leader, reading it can certainly use that information to figure out whether or not their mentor is a sponsor or a regular ordinary mentor. However, that same information can also be used by leaders to become sponsors of future leaders themselves. Choose to mentor others if you can because the process is so deeply rewarding, and let's face it, a leader cannot be a leader forever. Not even The Master from BtVS could be leader permanently even if one disregards Buffy and the Scooby Gang's part in stopping him. The key is to be a mentor who truly wants his or her mentees to grow into being effective leaders themselves. So, to put it in into a neat old Doublemeat Medley burger, anyone wanting to be an effective leader must be involved in mentorship, be it as a mentor or a mentee, and that mentorship should be ideally in terms of being a sponsor, an active one. Think Mayor Wilkins if he weren't an evil individual – that's the kind of active sponsor one should be striving to be for one's mentees and to have in one's life as a mentor.

SUMMARY

This chapter presents information about mentorship and uses several BtVS examples and situations to illustrate the benefits of mentoring, be it as a mentor or a mentee. I discuss the importance of being authentic while being involved as a mentor or as a mentee with a mentor. I also discuss the ways in which an individual can get started being involved in mentorship. I finally then discuss how a mentor can be a sponsor – it all boils down to being willing to sponsor your mentee into a position of power. In the next chapter, we are going to inject a bit of soul into the proceedings and learn about how both heart and soul are essential for effective leaders.

REFERENCES

1. Whedon, J., Batali, D., & Des Hotel, R. (Writers), & Green, B. S. (Director). (1997). The dark age (Season 2, Episode 8) [TV episode]. In *Buffy the Vampire Slayer*. Mutant Enemy Productions.

2. Shandley, T. C. (1989). The use of mentors for leadership development. *NASPA Journal*, 27(1), 59–66.

3. Shek, D. T., & Lin, L. (2015). Leadership and mentorship: Service leaders as mentors of the followers. *International Journal on Disability and Human Development*, 14(4), 351–359.

4. Daresh, J. C. (2001). *Leaders helping leaders: A practical guide to administrative mentoring*. Corwin Press.

5. McCorkle, L. S., Diamond, L. L., Yang, H. W., & Swindell, J. (2024). Preparing future leaders: What should we know about mentoring? *Mentoring & Tutoring: Partnership in Learning*, 32(1), 6–28.

6. Chao, G. T., Walz, P., & Gardner, P. D. (1992). Formal and informal mentorships: A comparison on mentoring functions and contrast with nonmentored counterparts. *Personnel Psychology*, 45(3), 619–636.

7. Ragins, B. R., & Cotton, J. L. (1999). Mentor functions and outcomes: A comparison of men and women in formal and informal mentoring relationships. *Journal of Applied Psychology*, 84(4), 529.

8. Raabe, B., & Beehr, T. A. (2003). Formal mentoring versus supervisor and coworker relationships: Differences in perceptions and impact. *Journal of Organizational Behavior*, 24(3), 271–271.

9. Petrie, D. (Writer), & Lang, M. (Director). (1999). Bad girls (Season 3, Episode 14) [TV episode]. In *Buffy the Vampire Slayer*. Mutant Enemy Productions.

10. Goddard, D. (Writer), & Solomon, D. (Director). (2002). Selfless (Season 7, Episode 5) [TV episode]. In *Buffy the Vampire Slayer*. Mutant Enemy Productions.

11. Greenberg, D. Z. (Writer), & Gershman, M. (Director). (2002). Him (Season 7, Episode 6) [TV episode]. In *Buffy the Vampire Slayer*. Mutant Enemy Productions.

12. Petrie, D. (Writer & Director). (2003). Get it done (Season 7, Episode 15) [TV episode]. In *Buffy the Vampire Slayer*. Mutant Enemy Productions.

13. Bell, A., & Treleaven, L. (2011). Looking for professor right: Mentee selection of mentors in a formal mentoring program. *Higher Education, 61*, 545–561.

14. Bartunek, J. M., Kram, K. E., Coffey, R., Lenn, D. J., Moch, M. K., & O'Neill, H. (1997). A group mentoring journey into the department chair role. *Journal of Management Inquiry, 6*(4), 270–279.

15. Goerisch, D., Basiliere, J., Rosener, A., McKee, K., Hunt, J., & Parker, T. M. (2019). Mentoring with: Reimagining mentoring across the university. *Gender, Place & Culture, 26*(12), 1740–1758.

16. Hewlett, S. A. (2013). *Forget a mentor, find a sponsor: The new way to fast-track your career*. Harvard Business Review Press.

17. Pfeffer, J. (2013). You're still the same: Why theories of power hold over time and across contexts. *Academy of Management Perspectives, 27*(4), 269–280.

18. Pfeffer, J. (2022). *7 Rules of power: Surprising–but true–advice on how to get things done and advance your career*. BenBella Books.

19. Pfeffer, J., & Fong, C. T. (2005). Building organization theory from first principles: The self-enhancement motive and understanding power and influence. *Organization Science, 16*(4), 372–388.

20. Noxon, M. (Writer), & Gershman, M. (Director). (1999). Consequences (Season 3, Episode 14) [TV episode]. In *Buffy the Vampire Slayer*. Mutant Enemy Productions.

21. Fandom. (n.d.). *Clement*. Buffyverse Wiki. Retrieved January 18, 2024, from https://buffy.fandom.com/wiki/Clement

22. Whedon, J. (Writer & Director). (1998). Becoming, Part 2 (Season 2, Episode 22) [TV episode]. In *Buffy the Vampire Slayer*. Mutant Enemy Productions.

5

ANGELUS TO ANGEL – (HEART AND) SOUL MATTERS

As we move into the fifth chapter of this book, I figured it might be time to write a bit more about Angel and Angelus – two sides of a different coin, so to speak. As most viewers of BtVS will know, Angel was a mainstay during the first two seasons, and at times, would be a protagonist, and at times, would be an antagonist. The switch between being a protagonist and antagonist literally involved his soul. When he was soulless, he was an evil bloodsucking villain of a vampire named Angelus – when the soul was in him, he'd be transformed into Angel, a vampire who Buffy and many in the Scooby Gang relied on. It was all a matter of whether or not his soul was missing or available.

To me the topic that comes to mind immediately when thinking about heart and soul is authenticity or to be specific, authentic leadership. This is one of the most popular types of leadership out there, and my bet is, if someone were to ask a random person what sort of leader they were, most of those asked would claim to be authentic leaders (regardless of whether or not they truly are authentic leaders). There are authentic leaders galore in the BtVS world, some we'd call heroic and others we'd call villains, but they all possessed a good modicum of authenticity.

In this chapter, I will begin by discussing what exactly authenticity and authentic leadership involve. After that, I will delve into the advantages and disadvantages (although, the ratio between the pros and cons will be a trifle bit lopsided) of being an authentic leader. Following that, I will discuss how exactly an individual can become or manifest himself or herself into being an authentic leader, while taking precautions to avoid the pitfalls of being an authentic leader. As has been the norm in previous chapters and will be in future chapters, I will illustrate all of this by using several examples and incidents from BtVS to help further drive the stake... I mean point home. So, let's start off with authenticity and authentic leadership first, shall we.

AUTHENTICITY

It stands to reason that prior to discussing authentic leadership, one must understand what authenticity refers to. In some ways, it would be akin to binge watching the BtVS series in reverse – while, I have no doubts, some people may enjoy the surreal experience, most will find it bewildering, and possibly resembling the confused rationale Xander used to ditch his wedding with Anya. Ah, what could have been... but anyway, one must know what authenticity is prior to discussing what the leadership style involving it is.

Authenticity is what we term as the attribute of an individual to act in accordance with his or her values and desires even if those values and desires go against social norms of conformity.[1-5] Consider Angel here – after he got cursed with the Ritual of Restoration by the Kalderash people when he was Angelus,[6] he ended up with a soul and the ability to feel remorse for his past actions. As Angel, he was scrupulous about not giving in to his natural Vampiric tendencies and instead mostly relied on animal blood for sustenance. Although to be fair, he did imbibe human blood, but only of who he considered to be morally reprehensible humans.

But as Angel, he could be classified as possessing a high degree of authenticity, especially when that sort of anti-vampiric behavior made him into a pariah of sorts with the vampire community at large. Compare Angel with Spike (with the chip in his brain), who couldn't attack humans to drink their blood. The difference between the two is that Angel chose to not attack normal humans and drink their blood, while Spike would have chosen that, but couldn't simply because the chip debilitated him. So, one could not classify Spike as authentic, not until season 7 anyway, when he got his soul back as well, and became truly or dare we say it, authentically harmless to ordinary normal human beings (who would previously be viewed purely as snack boxes).

Authenticity as a concept though has been viewed with some amount of skepticism in academic circles.[7-9] Critics have alleged that while there is a lot of surface agreement about what the term means, the reality is that different people use the term differently. For instance, some equate the term with the consistency between an entity's internal values and external expressions. Others equate the term with conformity of an entity with the norms of the social category the entity falls under. And then finally, others equate the term with the connection between an entity and a person, place, or time. As one can see from these differing conceptualizations, the entity need not be a person but could be an organization or a group, etc. But for the purposes of this chapter, I will be referring to authenticity from the perspective of it applying to an individual or a person.

Just to go a bit Gilesian here, to summarize, authenticity might sound like an easy and straightforward term to understand. However, as one can see, there are subtle nuances to it. Depending on who you're talking to or what you're talking about, the term could mean any of three possible conceptualizations. Having said that, as I mentioned in the last paragraph, I will be focusing on the consistency between the individual's internal values and manifested behaviors[10] as a definition of authenticity. This is what I will be basing my discussion on authentic leadership on. So, tally-ho, let's begin on the journey to understanding what authentic leadership entails.

AUTHENTIC LEADERSHIP

As I explained previously, authentic leadership basically involves the concept of authenticity in spadesful. Authentic leaders can be defined as individuals who are highly authentic in terms of knowing themselves and who they are and believing and acting on the values they hold. They are also transparent with others and never prevaricate in terms of their thought processes or behavior patterns. Of course, that does mean that on occasion, you're likely to run into individuals who don't quite fit the bill when it comes to your preconceived notions of what an authentic leader means.

Let's face it – most people would think of authentic leaders as positive forces. However, they can be negative forces as well. Think about the villains in the BtVS series – let's consider Adam, the undead biomechanical demonoid, who was a creation of Professor Maggie Walsh. Adam was pretty dang evil, of course; however, he was truly authentic. He spoke the truth and acted in accordance with what he believed. In terms of authentic leaders needing to truly know themselves, Adam really exemplified that principle. He was self-aware to the hilt and had a scientist's appetite for knowledge about himself and the world he existed in. So, by that yardstick, he was certainly authentic. Yes, his authenticity involved killing lots of innocent humans, but that inconvenient fact did not quite dent his authenticity.

Another individual from the BtVS series who could be said to be an authentic leader is Willow Rosenberg. I would also add that Tara MacLay was perhaps even more authentic in her own self-awareness than Willow, at least, in the beginning. Willow certainly grew in stature throughout the series – from being a diffident and underconfident girl in the beginning to becoming a powerful witch to becoming literally a badass villain as Dark Willow when she's grieving (this might be a spoiler here, so I'll try not to spoil it too much for people still catching up on BtVS). Let's just say Willow's grief changed her personality drastically for a while, till she eventually returned to being her usual lovable Willow self again, thanks to Xander's telling her repeatedly that he loves her no matter what.[11]

I talked about the above characters for a reason – I wanted to emphasize here that authentic leadership does not necessarily have to be only about positive or protagonist characters. It can have its negatives as well and, indeed, apply to antagonists as well. Villains can be authentic as well, after all, one can genuinely think vile thoughts and act on them. There is consistency between thought and action, isn't there? Think about dictators in our world, they would probably be fairly high in terms of authenticity. Their followers know exactly what to expect when it comes to interacting with those dictators, and there is likely congruence between the dictator's thinking and actions. It's not that a dictator has to pretend to be a nice and humble individual when they can afford to have an iron hand in an iron glove, with not a trace of velvet in the horizon.

Speaking of Xander, I might add that he also exemplifies authentic leadership, and quite well at that. Throughout the entire series, Xander is the one who is incredibly dependable and while that is played off for comic relief, he is literally the handyman of the Scooby Gang. He is quite skilled at not only repairing fixtures and broken windows but also repairing strife within the group. Honestly, without his authentic expression of love to Willow,[11] it is doubtful that Dark Willow could have reverted back to being lovable and kind Willow. Also, while I have previously complained about Joss Whedon's creative decision to have Xander walk out on Anya on their wedding day, one can see a bit of authenticity in Xander's actions, even then. When the demon Stewart Burns pretended to be Xander[12] from the future, he actually preyed on Xander's insecurity vis-à-vis his dysfunctional family. Xander was afraid that the familial trauma he suffered throughout his childhood and youth would be repeated by him when it came to Anya. The fictional future scene Stewart Burns showed Xander was realistic enough for him to understand that he simply wasn't confident in his own ability to overcome the generational trauma.

Now that I have discussed what exactly entails authenticity and provided some examples of authentic leaders from the BtVS series, let me get into some pros and cons of being an authentic leader.

PROS AND CONS OF BEING AUTHENTIC OR AN AUTHENTIC LEADER

One of the biggest pros of being authentic or an authentic leader is that you have to be transparent,[13-16] about your values and your intention. It is by default since the definition of authenticity sort of demands it. And that is certainly an advantage, because by being transparent, your followers no longer have to suffer constant anxiety by being worried about how you'll react. They will know exactly how to act and react to you. In a way, you will be more dependable and reliable and that will do wondrously to keep follower anxiety low. Another advantage of being an authentic leader is that you no longer have to engage in surface or deep acting.[17-20] Surface acting refers to when a person acts differently from what he or she thinks but knows that their behavior isn't genuine. In deep acting, a person tries to actively change their internal feelings to match with the behavior they're displaying. Both forms of acting can lead to emotional labor, but it is more pronounced with deep acting than surface acting.

Consider emotional labor[17,21-23] – that is basically one experiencing extreme cognitive dissonance since one has to behave in a way that is not concordant with how one feels. Both surface and deep acting are immensely damaging to an individual's psyche and mental health. There are a host of issues that individuals suffering from emotional labor face, and none of them are in the slightest bit beneficial. These issues include physical symptoms like migraines, fatigue, insomnia, emotional exhaustion, and even stomach problems.[23] Not exactly a pleasing proposition for anyone to have to undergo, and curiously, very reminiscent of when Spike had to act in a way discordant with what he wanted to do, thanks to the behavior modification circuitry chip embedded in his brain. One could liken emotional labor to Spike's situation then – you end up acting or behaving in a way that is completely at odds with what you want to truly do.

I have not had the misfortune of experiencing emotional labor and haven't had to do much if any surface or deep-level acting either, but I know friends and acquaintances who have. Their symptoms from facing emotional labor have been quite alarming to hear about, and sadly, it's not because they want to be inauthentic, but more so a function of the industry (hospitality/healthcare) they operate in. But regardless, I do think one of the biggest advantages of being authentic is that you end up avoiding the unfortunate aftermath of experiencing emotional labor. And to put a different spin on it, if you happen to embody authenticity, then your followers will too. They will not need to do any surface or deep-acting themselves.

However, it's not exclusively a bed of roses if you happen to be authentic or an authentic leader. One serious drawback to being highly authentic is that it can lead to rigidity of thought and an inexorable inflexibility. As a leader, that's the last thing you need to be. If you happen to be so convinced about your plans or strategies, and refuse to listen to dissenting voices because you want to be authentic, then perhaps, you should take a step back, and re-evaluate your position on the matter. There is being authentic to your thoughts and actions, and then there is being overly rigid and obstinate. The latter is one of the disadvantages of being overly authentic, and not logical enough.

Another disadvantage that I've seen some people display is choosing to be overly harsh while being authentic. One can be authentic and kind, even if delivering bad news, and yet, we have people out there who profess to be authentic leaders, and behave reprehensibly unkind. There is no necessity to be brutal, as one can still be authentic and kind. Why be a Principal Snyder when you could be a Principal Robin Wood instead? So, I'll just say that in the quest to be authentic, don't lose sight of the fact that you have to still work with and interact with fellow humans (well unless you're dealing with vampires or demons, of course), so why not be kind too? It doesn't cost a penny to be kind and yet be authentic.

Another aspect of authentic leadership that could be considered a disadvantage is that one person's authenticity is another person's poor behavior. This can directly be attributed to cultural and national differences. Take a country which has a culture that is high on assertiveness and compare it with another that is low on assertiveness. Individuals from the first culture will have a different understanding of authenticity than individuals from the second culture. Therefore, if you never tweak how you express your authenticity regardless of the cultural milieu you operate in, you may end up with an authenticity that repels others instead of attracting them.

DEVELOP YOURSELF INTO AN AUTHENTIC LEADER

Now that I've written a fair bit on what authenticity and authentic leadership mean and also discussed some of the advantages and disadvantages of being authentic or authentic leaders; it's time to discuss how an individual can develop oneself into an authentic leader. Now the diligent reader may see this and purse their lips, and inquire, why if I've discussed several disadvantages of authentic leaders and authenticity, do I have a section still on trying to develop people into authentic leaders? The answer to that is simply that there is practically nothing on this planet which can be said to be universally free of any disadvantages, and authenticity or authentic leadership is no exception. The advantages of being authentic yield much more desirable outcomes for us than do the demerits. So, it does, indeed, benefit us if we know how to develop into authentic leaders and increase our level of authenticity to an extent that we can minimize any possible disadvantages.

For starters, the first step to develop and hone one's authenticity is to truly know oneself. And I don't mean this in some sort of metaphysical way, but more so, in terms of getting to know one's own values. If you don't know what you truly stand for, you're not going to really know yourself. A good example from BtVS to help understand this is to remember when Spike gets his soul back.[11] Unlike Angelus, he's not cursed by anyone to get his soul back, but instead, he truly deeply desires it and is willing to suffer through a harsh ritual to get redemption and his soul back. He knows what he wants and is willing to suffer to get it. This is motivated in part because Spike had gotten to really love Buffy, and he was ashamed of his feral behavior toward her when he attempted a sexual assault. Spike did not ever want to do something as reprehensible as that again, and so he went in for that ritual, as hard as it was, even while understanding that the resultant remorse would likely drive him mad.

To know ourselves, we don't have to go through any such rigorous or painful rituals, all we have to do is figure out our values. Self-reflection is the way to go about doing that – you do have to be honest with yourself to come up with an accurate appraisal of your values. There are some assessments available that you could take, but it is also possible to come up with an assessment of your values by simply writing down what is important for you. Ask yourself questions like who you admire, what you want people to perceive you as, etc. Spike did something similar to this from the heart in order to get his soul back.

Once you've accurately identified your value system (and it might take more than just one sitting to do so), start by taking decisions that embody your value system. For instance, let's suppose that one of your values is that you will not touch a drop of alcohol (or human blood if you happen to be a vampire with a soul) – make sure to take decisions that respect and do not go contrary to your value. That means that you'll have to start skipping weekly bar bashes with work colleagues (sometimes sadly, these become rituals that force people to binge drink) even though that may dim your professional star, a little bit. However, there is no real point in eroding your own value system (by engaging in either surface or deep-level acting) just for a bit of career success. Be firm and stand your ground and protect yourself from having to engage in activities you don't agree with. There are also assessments for authentic leadership potential, which could be taken, and an individual could then identify weaknesses in their authentic leadership profile, which is another step toward increasing self-awareness.

So, just to emphasize here again – while, there are certainly some drawbacks at being overly authentic, in most circumstances the benefits of being authentic outweigh the drawbacks. Therefore, it makes perfect sense to strive to develop oneself as an authentic leader. It all begins with self-awareness and accurate appraisal of one's own values. Basically, one literally needs heart and soul when it comes to developing one's authenticity and potential for authentic leadership.

SUMMARY

This chapter discussed authenticity and authentic leadership and, in particular, defined what exactly authenticity implies. I also use several examples and situations from BtVS to explain these concepts. I discuss the pros and cons of being authentic or an authentic leader and then discuss how an individual can act to develop into an authentic leader themselves. As I've hinted throughout the chapter, both soul and heart are absolutely essential in becoming more authentic as a leader. In the next chapter, we are going to go the self-leadership route and discuss how that concept is super important for effective leaders.

REFERENCES

1. Kernis, M. H., & Goldman, B. M. (2006). A multicomponent conceptualization of authenticity: Theory and research. *Advances in Experimental Social Psychology, 38*, 283–357.

2. Goffee, R., & Jones, G. (2005). Managing authenticity. *Harvard Business Review, 83*(12), 85–94.

3. Ehman, R. R. (2012). *The authentic self.* Prometheus Books.

4. Reisinger, Y., & Steiner, C. J. (2006). Reconceptualizing object authenticity. *Annals of Tourism Research, 33*(1), 65–86.

5. Eagly, A. H. (2005). Achieving relational authenticity in leadership: Does gender matter? *The Leadership Quarterly, 16*(3), 459–474.

6. Whedon, J. (Writer & Director). (1998). Innocence (Season 2, Episode 14) [TV episode]. In *Buffy the Vampire Slayer.* Mutant Enemy Productions.

7. Shomoossi, N., & Ketabi, S. (2007). A critical look at the concept of authenticity. *Electronic Journal of Foreign Language Teaching, 4*(1), 149–155.

8. Lixinski, L. (2022). Against authenticity. *International Journal of Heritage Studies, 28*(11–12), 1213–1227.

9. Claviez, T., Imesch, K., & Sweers, B. (Eds.). (2020). *Critique of authenticity.* Vernon Press.

10. Hopwood, C. J., Good, E. W., Levendosky, A. A., Zimmermann, J., Dumat, D., Finkel, E. J., Eastwick, P. E., & Bleidorn, W. (2021). Realness is a core feature of authenticity. *Journal of Research in Personality, 92*, 104086.

11. Fury, D. (Writer), & Contner, J. A. (Director). (2002). Grave (Season 6, Episode 22) [TV episode]. In *Buffy the Vampire Slayer.* Mutant Enemy Productions.

12. Kirschner, R. (Writer), & Solomon, D. (Director). (2002). Hell's bells (Season 6, Episode 16) [TV episode]. In *Buffy the Vampire Slayer*. Mutant Enemy Productions.

13. Avolio, B. J., & Gardner, W. L. (2005). Authentic leadership development: Getting to the root of positive forms of leadership. *The Leadership Quarterly*, *16*(3), 315–338.

14. Kempster, S., Iszatt-White, M., & Brown, M. (2019). Authenticity in leadership: Reframing relational transparency through the lens of emotional labour. *Leadership*, *15*(3), 319–338.

15. Jiang, H., & Shen, H. (2023). Toward a relational theory of employee engagement: Understanding authenticity, transparency, and employee behaviors. *International Journal of Business Communication*, *60*(3), 948–975.

16. Rego, A., Cunha, M. P. E., & Giustiniano, L. (2022). Are relationally transparent leaders more receptive to the relational transparency of others? An authentic dialog perspective. *Journal of Business Ethics*, *180*(2), 695–709.

17. Mesmer-Magnus, J. R., DeChurch, L. A., & Wax, A. (2012). Moving emotional labor beyond surface and deep acting: A discordance–congruence perspective. *Organizational Psychology Review*, *2*(1), 6–53.

18. Grandey, A. A. (2003). When "the show must go on": Surface acting and deep acting as determinants of emotional exhaustion and peer-rated service delivery. *Academy of Management Journal*, *46*(1), 86–96.

19. Hill, N. S., Zhang, H., Zhang, X., & Ziwei, Y. (2020). The impact of surface and deep acting on employee creativity. *Creativity Research Journal*, *32*(3), 287–298.

20. Hoffmann, E. A. (2016). Emotions and emotional labor at worker-owned businesses: Deep acting, surface acting, and genuine emotions. *The Sociological Quarterly*, *57*(1), 152–173.

21. Brotheridge, C. M., & Lee, R. T. (2003). Development and validation of the emotional labour scale. *Journal of Occupational and Organizational Psychology*, *76*(3), 365–379.

22. Taylor, S. (1998). Emotional labour and the new workplace. *Workplaces of the Future*, 84–103.

23. Elliott, C. (2017). Emotional labour: Learning from the past, understanding the present. *British Journal of Nursing*, *26*(19), 1070–1077.

6

SELF-LEADERSHIP: CUES FROM THE SCOOBY GANG

After blazing through the first five chapters, here we are squarely in the middle of this book. In this sixth chapter, I'm going to be focusing on self-leadership. This particular concept may sound a bit oxymoronish, but it's really not. Self-leadership is a unique way of looking at leadership; in that, it essentially works to elevate individuals who don't have formal roles of leadership into acting as leaders. Therefore, for this chapter, I am going to be focusing a lot of attention on the Scooby Gang, that is, the members of it, that includes Anya, Xander, Willow, Oz, Tara, Dawn, etc. I suppose there'll be some mention of Buffy, Spike, and Giles too, but I will try to base more examples and proffer my explanation on the other Scoobies.

In this chapter, I will start off by defining and discussing self-leadership, especially since it does take a bit of reframing to understand self-leadership. I will also briefly discuss how exactly self-leadership often manifests. After that discussion, I will then discuss whether or not self-leadership is something that formal leaders ought to be encouraging or if caution needs to be adhered to. Following that section, I will then discuss ways by which individuals can start to improve their own self-leadership skills. I will illustrate all of these concepts with examples from the BtVS world, and as previously stated, these examples are going to be Scooby Gang heavy.

So, let's proceed to describe and discuss what exactly self-leadership is, and under what circumstances, it typically begins to arise. In some ways, one could compare it to a new vampire rising from the grave. Sometimes, in a couple of hours, and other times, almost immediately. But typically, it's an overnight process. Similarly, self-leadership takes a bit of overnight stewing, prior to rising. And, while this is not exactly a perfect metaphor, it works; I think to put forth the point that self-leadership often springs up when it's least anticipated.

SELF-LEADERSHIP: WHAT IS IT?

Okay, on to the raison d'etre of this particular chapter – what exactly is self-leadership? A technical (if somewhat overly academic and stuffy) definition is that self-leadership is a process of influencing oneself and allowing oneself to possess self-direction and self-motivation.[1-4] In simpler terms (so as to not resemble a spell being cast by Jonathan from the oh so nefarious Trio), self-leadership involves an individual (or team) motivating and providing direction to themselves, without needing any prodding from an external leader.

When you look at the Scooby Gang, several of the characters in it demonstrate their self-leadership skills throughout the series. Let's start off with Dawn (I just realized that up until this point, I have not really discussed a whole lot about Dawn), so it is only fair to do so now. As we know Dawn was the Key in the beginning, just a mystical power source of sorts, who gets embedded into the Summers' lives by the surviving members of the Order of Dagon.[5] She's basically the baby sister of the group and, more often than not, is somewhat ignored, or at least, her inputs and insights aren't taken very seriously by Buffy or anyone else (except for Spike and perhaps Xander, I should add here). In fact, if you look at some of the chatter on online Buffy forums, Dawn tends to be mostly ignored if not disliked by a lot of fans. Which is a bit unfortunate, because while she isn't my favorite character, she still played an important role in the series.

One example of a time when Dawn displays serious self-leadership skills is when she pretty much takes on the researcher role in the group. She is the one who finds the information about Gnarl,[6] the demon that paralyzes its victims, skins them to eat strips of their flesh at leisure, and also drinks the blood of its victims. So, a rather gnarly demon, with a befitting name – that information wouldn't have been obtained had it not been for Dawn's insistence that they search for demons with a penchant for skinning victims. Buffy didn't even think that was a worthwhile pursuit to do, so Dawn certainly demonstrated excellent self-leadership in that instance.

Now, let's shift gears a bit and talk about Tara. She's another character that is pretty squarely in a supportive role throughout the series. While she's kind and dependable, she isn't really a main character (although she is sort of responsible for Willow's transformation into Dark Willow). So, even though she's never really the main character, she still is a very important one and has demonstrated self-leadership on many occasions. One prominent instance is the one where she actually finds the spell that helps the entire population of the town of Sunnydale to get their voices back[7] (which they'd lost due to the polite fairy tale villains, the Gentlemen, who stole voices in order to cut out their hearts). Without Tara's display of self-leadership during this time, it is highly improbable that the Gentlemen could have ever been defeated.

This also kicks off the start to the budding romance between Tara and Willow, and Tara certainly shows her self-leadership several times throughout the series – another poignant display of self-leadership is when she willingly makes the decision to separate from Willow because the latter was getting too attached and addicted to dangerous and risky magic. Tara shows that she possesses enough self-motivation and self-direction to be able to exit a toxic relationship that seems to be getting worse.[8] In many ways, it's almost like a relationship where one partner gets addicted to a substance (in this case, dark magic), and the other partner tries to get them to recover, but the addicted partner refuses to receive help. In such circumstances, the partner who isn't addicted should think about their own wellbeing and exit, which is what Tara did. One simply cannot help a person who isn't willing to receive the help or to act on concrete steps that are necessary. The ability to exit a toxic or irreparable relationship where one partner simply isn't seeing reason demonstrates good self-leadership skills.

Now, I'm going to go on to the next section which will discuss the circumstances under which self-leadership often is manifested. After all, it doesn't simply arise up without any reason – there is always something that brings it out, so let's get to discussing how exactly self-leadership is manifested.

HOW IS SELF-LEADERSHIP MANIFESTED?

So, essentially there are three main categories of self-leadership tactics, one of which is focused on behavior focused strategies, and another is natural reward strategies, and the third is through constructive thought pattern strategies. Any of these strategies can help individuals develop their own self-leadership skills. Behavior focused strategies focus on changing one's behavior in order to improve any area that you may think you are deficient in. The perfect example here to discuss is Willow. In the beginning, she was shown as a rather underconfident and shy person, who is super smart, but just very unsure about herself. She ends up becoming a dominant force of power in the later seasons of the show, and that's not just automatically, but instead quite consciously due to Willow's desire to change. One of the highpoints of Willow shedding her shy nature aside can be seen in the way that she took charge in the resurrection of Buffy,[9] after Buffy died in the previous season[10] during the battle with Glory (in order to seal the portal that had opened up). Without Willow leading the initiative to resurrect Buffy, BtVS may have ended in a rather untimely fashion after season 5.

These behavior-focused self-leadership tactics usually involve goal-setting and that too can be seen to fit Willow, especially as she worked on improving her prowess in magic and spellcasting throughout the BtVS series. But another Scooby Gang member also fits the bill really well here. I refer to Anya, or the previously demonic vengeance demon Anyanka. When Anyanka turns into the human Anya, she is determined to learn more on how to be human. Even though she really lacks the ability to understand human emotions like love or friendship, she strives to do her best to understand them better in order to have a better relationship with Xander. Additionally, she is super motivated to become financially independent and shows a great deal of initiative and zeal during her time at the Magic Box. Eventually, she even takes over the store from Giles and that serves to showcase how much she grows from being a naïve new human to a seasoned business proprietor.

Another example of a Scooby Gang member who displayed great self-leadership and initiative throughout his time there is Riley. He was certainly the most human among Buffy's boyfriends, and while he did suffer from occasional bouts of inadequacy especially when comparing his own ordinary humanity with Buffy's own elevated humanity. However, he recognizes that he needs to improve himself and choses to leave Sunnydale and rebuild his own life, even getting married to another demon hunter, Samantha Finn. Riley was certainly driven and established goals to accomplish, one of which involved getting out of the initiative, especially because they were experimenting on him with ability enhancing medicine and also had a behavior modification chip in his chest (which Riley was able to cut out with a shard of glass).

When it comes to natural reward strategies,[3] I can think of nobody better than Oz (or Daniel Osbourne) who was Willow's first boyfriend. The duo broke up because each individual suspected infidelity on the other's part (and with good reason, if I must say so). And then Oz leaves town, so he was no longer a part of the Scooby Gang. But when he was part of the gang, he certainly did display some good self-leadership. He was one of the few werewolves out there who took care to not go out on mindless hunts and was self-aware enough to lock himself up in a cage during full moon nights. Additionally, as far as natural reward strategies are concerned, Oz invites the Scooby Gang to come watch his band *Dingoes Ate My Baby* perform. That invite could be interpreted as a natural reward of sorts, as it basically fulfills the role of adding pleasant activities to the group. A win-win of sorts, as Oz liked to perform, and the Scooby Gang liked to hear the band's performance.

The third category, namely constructive thought pattern strategies,[11-13] is pretty much reserved as the forte of Xander (to be fair, Dawn takes on a little bit of this role toward the end in the last two seasons). But Xander is pretty much consistent throughout the series as being the one Scooby Gang member who could always be relied on to bring a bit of levity and optimism to the discussion, no matter how heavy or dark it may have been. Xander does feel a bit inadequate at times, due to not having any supernatural or super powers, when compared to other Scooby Gang members. And one could certainly argue that his humor and ability to joke even during serious circumstances is a coping mechanism. However, Xander does not do this coping without knowing about it – he pretty much knows that his humor is a coping mechanism. But he still finds the self-motivation to keep being the reliable steadfast sans power ordinary member of the group. When he praises Dawn for being so tranquil even when she is so disappointed that she's not a potential slayer, he actually gets praised back by Dawn, who tells him that his superpower is the ability to notice things that others are oblivious to.[14]

That touching interaction between the two is a perfect example of how Xander not only practices constructive thought patterns himself but is also able to get others to similarly start thinking constructive thoughts themselves. On several occasions, he's also caused several of the other Scooby Gang members to revise their somewhat gloomy thought patterns, to become more positive. In short, Xander truly has the superpower to engage in constructive thought patterns and even get other people to change their own thinking. In some ways, you could say that self-leadership can help in making other people improve their self-leadership skills. This is a great point to segue to the next section, which will discuss whether or not formal leaders should be encouraging their followers to develop their self-leadership skills.

SHOULD LEADERS BE ENCOURAGING THEIR FOLLOWERS TO DEVELOP SELF-LEADERSHIP SKILLS?

This may be sounding like one of those science headlines where a person reading them smacks their own face and mutters how obvious it really is. And truly, to an extent, it does sound very obvious. I mean, why wouldn't formal leaders want their followers to develop their own self-leadership skills? After all, self-leadership is something worthwhile pursuing, and you also end up with followers who can eventually become leaders themselves. So, it sounds like a super neat deal, right? After all, who could resist having followers who are self-directed, and self-motivated, and self-led? And, it does really have a lot of advantages and benefits – for instance, studies have found that self-leadership is associated with higher levels of self-efficacy as well as increased performance. Indeed, it has been proposed that the trio are linked together with self-efficacy being a mediator between self-leadership and performance.

So, with those advantages, one can see that leaders who provide their followers with high degrees of empowerment are in a sense allowing them to develop and hone their self-leadership skills. There are lots of positives when it comes to empowering followers – first is that if you empower someone, that individual or group is a lot more likely than unempowered individuals or groups to be enthusiastic and engaged at work. Disengaged employees are the ones who mechanically and disinterestedly do their work, and while the work may be passable, there really is no heart in it. At times in BtVS, we see individuals being super dispirited and disengaged; one prominent character who quite exemplified that disengagement was Cordelia, especially in the beginning season. She eventually comes around and becomes a more engaged and useful member of the Scooby Gang.

But there is one drawback that can arise if leaders spend a lot of time and effort in empowering their followers. That drawback is simply that if employees are overly empowered then there is a risk of the leader's power and ability to influence eroding. Empowered employees could engage in both functional and dysfunctional resistance, and while the former is certainly preferable to the latter, it still doesn't make the leader's job any easier. A perfect example to illustrate this is during the final season, when Buffy and the Scooby Gang have to host the many potential slayers, in order to protect them from the murderous Caleb. In the beginning, Buffy is the chosen one, but when confronted with the possibility of three dozen or so potential slayers, and the reemergence of Faith, things do get a bit dicey.

In fact, Buffy's leadership is spurned by the potential slayers who feel a lot more empowered by the freer spirited and somewhat more irresponsible but fun Faith's style, as compared to the more serious and straight-laced Buffy style. Additionally, even Dawn asks Buffy to leave, since she's just not willing to accept that the group wanted to follow Faith's leadership at this point.[15] In a way, this example illustrates one major pitfall of leaders empowering or encouraging their followers to increase their levels of self-leadership. Sounds a bit like someone training an AI algorithm to do their job, doesn't it? Eventually, the algorithm could become empowered enough to no longer need you.

But of course, I don't want this section to sound like a doomsday prediction and rail against leaders encouraging their followers to increase their self-leadership levels. That is absolutely not the intention here – but I do wish to provide a bit of caution to anyone thinking about going in the whole hog with empowerment. If you over-empower, you may be rendering yourself obsolete in the long run. After all, if everyone is a leader, why would any group or organization need a formal leader. And sometimes if everyone is empowered, you could run into issues of decision paralysis, where you do need a strong leader to corral the group into deciding on action for the benefit of all. Now, I will discuss how a person can improve his or her own self-leadership.

HOW DO YOU IMPROVE YOUR SELF-LEADERSHIP?

Like most concepts in leadership, we really have to consider self-awareness. You have to know yourself, as Socrates would say. Prior to embarking on a plan to develop your self-leadership skills, invest some time to find out which self-leadership tactic or skill, you should be focusing on. Different individuals will have different strengths and weaknesses – for instance, take Cordelia. In the beginning, she's not super likeable – pretty much the archetype of a mean girl in school. But then eventually, the fake drama in such petty matters gets to be too stifling for even Cordelia. That's when she truly begins to develop her self-leadership, when she realizes that the Scooby Gang might not be the most popular group in high school, but they are instead incredibly important in keeping the denizens of Sunnydale alive. She also even manages to contribute to the Scooby's missions on several occasions, and especially during the events on their graduation day, Cordelia manages to stake her first vampire.[16] I would argue that this development in Cordelia's character is a direct result of her growing self-awareness of her own behavior, as well as better recognition of others' relatively kind treatment of her. This self-awareness helps her gain the necessary impetus to be self-directed.

Another great way to improve your own self-leadership is to engage in constructive thought patterns, or in other words, be more optimistic. Hope and optimism are certainly great allies in the quest to improve self-leadership. If an individual is despondent, then there isn't going to be a whole lot of self-leadership emerging from that person. Think of the time when Buffy runs away from home[17] and ends up in Los Angeles (and well, also runs into and eventually ends the enslaving demon, Ken). But when she's feeling all despondent, her slayer skills also suffer. Also, I must point out here that when Buffy is A.W.O.L., the rest of the Scooby Gang sans Angel tries to take up the mantle of duty and do her nightly patrols (with decidedly mixed and inferior results) – so, in a sense, a missing leader can also help followers develop self-leadership skills.

And then, one must always remember to focus on the positive aspects of one's job. There are positive aspects of work and negative aspects of work, and while one shouldn't develop amnesia about the negative aspects of one's work, one shouldn't let that overwhelm one's overall feelings about work. Concentrate on the positives of your job or work and that will help you perform so much better. Additionally, perception is reality, so if you focus on the positive aspects of your job, your job and your resultant work will become a lot more pleasant. Of course, this does not mean that you ignore toxic environments while focusing on the positive aspects – there obviously has to be a balanced approach here, in that, if the toxicity exceeds the pleasant aspects, then no point in sticking out there. Be like Spike and Drusilla, and get out of that particular job – you don't have to go to South America of course, but if you do, it's a lovely part of the world to go to.

So, all in all, it isn't too insurmountable to improve your own self-leadership skills. And in many ways, it can be a positive beneficial thing to do. By demonstrating your prowess in self-leadership, you are basically signaling to the world that you're ready and willing to take on actual formal leadership roles. Just be cautious not to get too bogged down in positive thinking that you completely ignore the obviously hazardous element in your job. For instance, being appointed as principal of Sunnydale High might have its high points, but one should be sure to not forget that the school is rather too uncomfortably close to a literal hellmouth, in fact, right beneath the library, so it comes with plenty of dangerous life-threatening challenges. Self-leadership does not mean you ignore all of that and only focus on the perks of being a principal.

SUMMARY

This chapter introduced self-leadership and discussed what exactly self-leadership is. I also discussed how self-leadership is actually manifested. Following that, I also discussed the pros and cons of self-leadership, as in, whether formal leaders ought to encourage it or not. I finally concluded with how individuals can improve their own self-leadership skills while being cognizant that they shouldn't be overdoing it. I illustrated all of these sections with examples from BtVS, and as promised in the beginning, I did try to focus on the Scooby Gang follower members as opposed to the more leader-like members. In the next chapter, I will discuss leader identity, and our good friend "Big Bad" or "William the Bloody" will be featured rather well in that particular chapter. So, let's all recite a bad poem using the word, and rouse ourselves from harsh repose, and bustle along to the next chapter.

REFERENCES

1. Stewart, G. L., Courtright, S. H., & Manz, C. C. (2019). Self-leadership: A paradoxical core of organizational behavior. *Annual Review of Organizational Psychology and Organizational Behavior*, 6(1), 47–67.

2. Harari, M. B., Williams, E. A., Castro, S. L., & Brant, K. K. (2021). Self-leadership: A meta-analysis of over two decades of research. *Journal of Occupational and Organizational Psychology*, 94(4), 890–923.

3. Manz, C. C. (1986). Self-leadership: Toward an expanded theory of self-influence processes in organizations. *Academy of Management Review*, 11(3), 585–600.

4. Ntshingila, N., Downing, C., & Hastings-Tolsma, M. (2021, April). A concept analysis of self-leadership: The "bleeding edge" in nursing leadership. *Nursing Forum*, 56(2), 404–412.

5. Petrie, D. (Writer), & Solomon, D. (Director). (2000). No place like home (Season 5, Episode 5) [TV episode]. In *Buffy the Vampire Slayer*. Mutant Enemy Productions.

6. Espenson, J. (Writer), & Contner, J. A. (Director). (2002). Same time, same place (Season 7, Episode 3) [TV episode]. In *Buffy the Vampire Slayer*. Mutant Enemy Productions.

7. Whedon, J. (Writer & Director). (1999). Hush (Season 4, Episode 10) [TV episode]. In *Buffy the Vampire Slayer*. Mutant Enemy Productions.

8.Kirshner, R. R. (Writer), & Grossman, D. (Director). (2001). Tabula rasa (Season 6, Episode 8) [TV episode]. In *Buffy the Vampire Slayer*. Mutant Enemy Productions.

9. Noxon, M. (Writer), & Grossman, D. (Director). (2001). Bargaining (Season 6, Episode 1) [TV episode]. In *Buffy the Vampire Slayer*. Mutant Enemy Productions.

10. Whedon, J. (Writer & Director). (2001). The gift (Season 5, Episode 22) [TV episode]. In *Buffy the Vampire Slayer*. Mutant Enemy Productions.

11. Houghton, J. D., & Jinkerson, D. L. (2007). Constructive thought strategies and job satisfaction: A preliminary examination. *Journal of Business and Psychology*, 22, 45–53.

12. Watkins, E. R. (2008). Constructive and unconstructive repetitive thought. *Psychological Bulletin*, 134(2), 163.

13. Epstein, S., & Meier, P. (1989). Constructive thinking: A broad coping variable with specific components. *Journal of Personality and Social Psychology*, 57(2), 332.

14. Kirshner, R. R. (Writer), & Contner, J. A. (Director). (2003). Potential (Season 7, Episode 12) [TV series episode]. In *Buffy the Vampire Slayer*. Mutant Enemy Productions; 20th Century Fox Television.

15. Greenberg, D. Z. (Writer), & Contner, J. A. (Director). (2003). Empty places (Season 7, Episode 19) [TV series episode]. In *Buffy the Vampire Slayer*. Mutant Enemy Productions; 20th Century Fox Television.

16. Whedon, J. (Writer/Director). (1999). Graduation Day, Part 2 (Season 3, Episode 22) [TV series episode]. In *Buffy the Vampire Slayer*. Mutant Enemy Productions; 20th Century Fox Television.

17. Whedon, J. (Writer/Director). (1999). Anne (Season 3, Episode 1) [TV series episode]. In *Buffy the Vampire Slayer*. Mutant Enemy Productions; 20th Century Fox Television.

7

A SPIKEY PATH TO LEADER IDENTITY

Seven is a lucky number, or at least, is perceived by most people to be a lucky number. Notice the modifier "most" since even seven is not universally acknowledged as being lucky. In the Chinese lunar calendar for instance, the seventh month is termed as the Hungry Ghost Festival month, or the month when the gates of Hell are open, and ghosts are free to roam and romp around on Earth. Sounds a tad bit similar to our Halloween, except in BtVS where Vampires and Demons take the day off. If you recall the episode *Halloween*[1] in BtVS, where thanks to the spell by Ethan, the Scooby Gang gets changed into the characters of the costumes they're wearing (so, Xander becomes a soldier while Willow becomes a ghost). In a sense, the spell causes our heroic trio (remember it was still early days back then, so it's just the core trio, Buffy, Willow, and Xander) whose identities take on the identities that their costumes would typically have.

Identity is an interesting concept – we all have multiple identities we wrestle with and, in some cases, have to sometimes choose one identity over another in quick succession. Think about an individual who works with their spouse in the same organization. At work, their interactions will be different and involve different identities than will their interactions at home. The same applies for leadership, as there are multiple identities leaders also need to wrestle with. It is important to be able to skillfully maneuver and use these various identities, and at times, like a ventriloquist, be able to project the image of the identity you want to portray.

In this chapter, I will discuss what identity really means, and how many layers or levels it operates in. Following that I will discuss leader identity specifically, in terms of how leaders can build and project their identities, in order to get followers to be influenced by them. I will also discuss how to avoid overidentification. The goal is, of course, to become an effective leader, not just play a game of identity musical chairs. And in this chapter, as the title suggests, I am going to be mostly discussing Spike from BtVS – there are so many layers in his character that I think doing a deep dive into that alone is going to be interesting. But of course, if a few other characters pop in for a bit, that should be fine too. After all, the goal is to understand leader identity through examples of situations and characters from BtVS. So, let's go on to discuss what identity means.

THE "IDENTITY" OF IDENTITY AND ITS COMPONENTS

Scholars have argued that there are narrow and broad ways of looking at identity, where the former ways involve looking at one's own feelings about one's own self and one's self-definition and one's own values.[2-6] The broader way though happens to focus on skills, abilities, and behaviors. Both the narrow and broader ways of looking at identity make up the entirety of the concept of identity. Let's talk about Spike in this context now – in the beginning, when he first appears on BtVS[7] with a slightly (well okay, more than slightly) insane Drusilla, the identity he possesses is that of a cocksure yet charming vampire. His charming looks and bad boy attitude are enough to persuade and fool lots of potential victims, who buy into that sense of identity which he projects. However, when you drill down to it, Spike's identity is a rather multifaceted entity – even in the beginning, when he's all bad-boy attituded, he is surprisingly loyal and devoted to the insane Drusilla. One could say kind even and that is not something his projected identity supports. This brings us to the various levels inherent in identity, which comprise the overall description.

The first level of identity is individual and independent identity.[8-9] This level is focused on one's own sense of understanding of individual traits and characteristics. Spike had a very good understanding of his own individual traits and characteristics, which you'll see is deliberate. His vampire bad-boy persona was a direct contradiction to his human persona. William Pratt in the late 1800s was a far cry from William the Bloody, who is a brash, confident, and arrogant individual. The original William Pratt was a socially awkward and sensitive human, who seemed to be overly reliant on his mother.[10] Indeed, if the bad boy vampire Spike was the one reciting his bad poetry in the 1800s, it is probable that the poetry would have received decent amounts of plaudits and praise.

Identity does matter, even the identity that one projects. That brings us to the next level of identity, which is interpersonal and relational identity.[9,11–12] This form of identity has to do with one's interdependent relationship with another individual, be it a romantic partner or a coworker or a supervisor. In the case of Spike, you can see how this level of identity also is a really important layer of his identity. When he was human, he wanted people to identify him as a flourishing and polished poet. He expresses his love for Cecily with a poem, but that poem is cruelly received by her and others, which also causes them give him the cruel moniker of "William the Bloody" for his bloody awful poetry.[10] And to top it all, Cecily rejects him and even calls him beneath her status. Essentially, at this stage in his life, his sense of interpersonal and relational identity is rather shattered. Which is why when Drusilla finds him disconsolate in a hay barn tearing up while tearing up his poetry, and is then kind to him, that creates a bit of a bond in him, which directly relates to how the future Spike's identity is heavily vested in social identity, or identity with a social group.

The third level of identity is collective and social identity.[9,13–15] This is the form of identity that is based off on membership in a social group. As was shown in BtVS, and also alluded to several times, Spike's human existence lacked much of a collective or social identity. He was shunned by the groups that he craved to be part of (the sort of people you would consider the in-crowd or the popular and upper-echelon class type of people). But then when he became a vampire after being sired by Drusilla, he ended up becoming part of a rather high-status high-class group of vampires (the Whirlwind as Darla referred to them in *Angel* – I realize I shouldn't be referring to a different show here, but this particular one is apt, so do please excuse this inclusion). Therefore, as Spike the vampire, his association with vampires was very much central to his identity. He does retain a certain upper-class sort of prejudice even as a vampire (i.e., he looks down upon weaker and lower status vampires), but his association with the collective group of vampires is a lot more important to him than was his association with other humans when he was human. But overall throughout the series, one can see these different layers of identity playing out.

Another layer of identity is the one conferred on people based off on cultural or national identity. This too you can see a bit more loosely than you do with most people, but you do see it with Spike. Recall his accent which could be said to be rather an affected cockney accent – the reality is that when he was human, he spoke in a more refined accent. The cockney accent is a fake one and is taken on in order to prove his bad boy credentials. After all Spike has been alive for hundreds of years, and yet, he continues to speak in his fake cockney accent. He could have easily obtained an American accent, like Angel did. While Angel was erstwhile Liam back in Ireland in the 18th century, he did spend a lot of time in the United States and that perhaps influenced his gradually adopting an American accent. Spike, on the other hand, continues to use his British accent to emphasize his British roots, possibly to showcase his identity based off cultural or national identity.

And then there is organizational identity, which refers to the identity of the organizations themselves, which, in turn, gives a certain shade of identity to the people embedded within the organization. From a BtVS perspective, people serving on the Watcher's Council could be said to have a starkly different identity than people serving in the Order of Aurelius. The latter you will remember was comprised entirely of vampires and that too vampires who thought of themselves as being elite. Come to think of it, the Watcher's Council crew also thought of themselves as being elite. So, that's one similarity between the members of two vastly different organizations.

LEADER IDENTITY

So, now that we've read a fairly lengthy discussion on the layered identity of Spike aka the erstwhile William Pratt, time to bring up the question of identity of leaders and in leadership. One way to see how identity affects leadership is to consider that leaders occupy a role, that is, they occupy the role of leader. And in that role, they have to use different identities at different times. A bit like Spike himself when you think of it. Spike's behavior with certain individuals was very different than his behavior with others. For instance, with Drusilla, he was actually very caring. However, with Harmony (who was his girlfriend for a short while), he was noticeably less caring and rather more acerbic in tone.[16] One could argue that the difference was because Spike had a natural affection and predilection for his sire, whereas in the case of Harmony, he has no such history with her, and so his annoyance with her is decidedly open.

As leaders, there are multiple identities that clash with each other. For instance, you might have a leader whose organizational identity clashes with their individual and independent identity. Think about someone who happens to be a rather self-important, pompous, and old-fashioned sort of individual who happens to be a leader in an organization, where the culture of the place is a lot more free-spirited and significantly more bohemian. If the leader tries to lead using their default independent identity, there will be a clash with other folks who work at that organization. So, they do have to pick and perhaps adapt layers of their identity when the situation demands it. Even if there's one layer of their identity that they really want to use in their decision-making, perhaps the situation at hand demands another layer of their identity to be utilized.

An example of the above can be seen several times in BtVS especially with Spike, who is a lot more adept at switching identities depending on the situation than is Angel. When we first see Spike, his big bad persona is the one that's showcased. But when he's essentially neutered by the initiative, and their "big bad" behavior modification circuitry; he turns to the Scooby Gang to try to initially survive because the chip is interfering with his ability to do so. While he comes in trying to intimidate them, he eventually has to resort to ingratiation to get what he wants. In a way, you can tell that the identity that works best with the Scooby Gang is the one which has an element of William Pratt's more gentle identity mixed in.

So, leaders do need to switch up their identities and, possibly, do so multiple times within the span of a single day. At times, they may need to showcase their individual identities, and at times, their national identity may be what's handy. Other times, it might be their organizational identity which needs to come into focus, and at times, their collective or social identity may be what's needed. Another aspect to consider here is that not only should leaders be judicious about using their own identities, they should also be cognizant about the effect of their identity portrayal on their followers. After all, so much research has shown that followers tend to imitate their leader's attitudes and behaviors that identity too may become something that followers end up imitating.

The aspect of clashing of identities which I mentioned a few paragraphs ago is an important aspect to consider. While indubitably true that some layers of identities may be more salient in some situations than others, the fact is that everyone has one primary layer of self-identity that shines through all of their various layers. For instance, one might be a generally kind individual, and even if that individual is in a role that demands assertiveness, perhaps that kindness will modify the level of assertiveness somewhat. However, another factor to consider here is the factor of authenticity. If one has to act in a way that is not consistent with one's self-identity, then there will be no authenticity. And as a result, then cognitive dissonance will follow, and life can get rather miserable after that.

The arc when Spike gets his soul back, thanks to his own desire to truly receive Buffy's forgiveness, is one that exemplifies what happens when identities clash. So, after Spike gets his soul back, he still continues to be a vampire, but now he's gotten his soul back, he also has the ability to strongly feel remorse. In fact, he practically goes crazy right after getting his soul back; however, when you compare that with what transpires with Angelus, you see there's definitely a significant difference. The difference is that Spike's getting his soul back was something he craved, and it was a reward essentially for having gone through the demon trials set by Lloyd.

Angelus, on the other hand, was cursed into having his soul restored, which is why suffered the consequences for a significantly longer time and, indeed, suffered longer. While Spike did become temporarily insane, part of that was also due to the fact that the First Evil also did its best to torture Spike then. In the case of Angelus, there wasn't any particular evil entity going after him. The very fact that he was cursed with soul restoration was enough torture for him, and Spike also benefited from the fact that Buffy stood up for him (despite the machinations by Principal Wood and Giles to kill Spike). That helped him weather the crisis caused by the return of his soul and the First Evil's resultant interference. Now let's move along to overidentification, which is something one shouldn't be trying to do.

OVERIDENTIFICATION WITH ANY IDENTITY LAYER

Now while it is, indeed, a good thing to accord importance to one's identity, it is also imperative not to overidentify with any aspect of identity.[9] This becomes particularly troublesome when one subsumes one's own identity and tacks it on to a leader or an organization's identity. For instance, consider the old stereotype of professors being absent minded and flaky souls. That may well be true for some folks but shouldn't be used as a lens of identity for all individuals who are professors. I know plenty of professors myself who are a far cry from the hackneyed stereotype. A good example of a character who certainly overidentified with a group or rather an element of her identity is Cordelia Chase.

As I've mentioned before, Cordy was the social queen of Sunnydale High School, and she certainly lived up to that facet of her identity as a popular but mean to unpopular people individual. In a sense, you could say that she overidentified with that facet of her identity. Even when she didn't really want to be mean, she ended up having to be mean in order to preserve her status as the queen of popular girls. This was particularly true during her interactions with good old Xander, where she was very hesitant to declare to the world that she was developing feelings for Xander. She basically overidentified with her identity in the group, to the extent of ignoring her true authentic independent identity.

Leaders ought to be on the guard too when it comes to overidentification. They need to resist the temptation to focus too much on any one identity, especially when there's a chance of identity clashes. They have to be able to optimize the selection of identity, in terms of choosing the right identity in a given situation or scenario. If they are out on a family vacation for instance, then activating the identity of a CEO is unlikely to yield a whole lot of joy for anyone. Instead, they should let their independent individual identity function the most, because after all, the vacation is time with their family, and the identity that should be most salient in a family situation is the independent individual identity. Being overly focused on your company or organization at all times is a recipe for disaster.

From that perspective, Spike is actually pretty good in terms of being able to use the most optimal version of his identity. He is actually fairly adept at picking the identity which works best with a given situation. When he's more or less neutered thanks to the brain modification circuitry, he is able to project the identity that allows the rest of the Scooby Gang to at least tolerate him, if not trust him fully. And similarly, when he's the anti-establishment rebellious Spike, he portrays that image and identity with enthusiasm. As I discussed previously, Spike is actually a lot more comfortable with his own multilayered identity than is Angel. That comfort helps him avoid the issue of overidentification that could otherwise creep in like an uninvited guest of the night. Similarly, leaders who are comfortable with their various identities are perhaps the best equipped to avoid overidentification or identity clash type situations.

SUMMARY

In this chapter, I present a discussion on identity, and the various layers that identity comprises of. This includes a discussion of the various identity components. I also discuss leader identity in terms of how leaders need to avoid a clash of identities in order to be able to optimize the best sort of identity for a given situation. I also discuss the peril of overidentification and discuss how it is important to not overidentify with any one sort of identity. One should be willing to switch identities depending on the need of the situation one happens to be in. All of the preceding concepts were discussed using Spike, with an occasional mention of a few other BtVS characters. Next chapter we are going to muster up a modicum of resilience and discuss resilience. One can expect to read about more BtVS characters in that chapter – it won't be a Spike heavy discussion like this one was.

REFERENCES

1. Ellsworth, C. (Writer), & Green, B. S. (Director). (1997). Halloween (Season 2, Episode 6) [TV series episode]. In *Buffy the Vampire Slayer*. Mutant Enemy Productions; 20th Century Fox Television.

2. Lounsbury, J. W., Levy, J. J., Leong, F. T., & Gibson, L. W. (2007). Identity and personality: The big five and narrow personality traits in relation to sense of identity. *Identity: An International Journal of Theory and Research*, 7(1), 51–70.

3. Van Knippenberg, D., Van Knippenberg, B., De Cremer, D., & Hogg, M. A. (2004). Leadership, self, and identity: A review and research agenda. *The Leadership Quarterly*, 15(6), 825–856.

4. Lord, R., & Hall, R. (2003). Identity, leadership categorisation, and leadership schema. In D. van Knippenberg & M. A. Hogg (Eds.), *Leadership and power: Identity processes in groups and organisations* (pp. 48–64). Sage.

5. Hogg, M. A. (2004). Social identity and leadership. In Messick, D. M., & R. M. Kramer (Eds.), *The psychology of leadership: New perspectives and research* (p. 53–80). Lawrence Erlbaum Associates Publishers.

6. Sinclair, A. (2011). Being leaders: Identities and identity work in leadership. *The Sage handbook of leadership*, 508–517.

7. Greenwalt, D. (Story & Teleplay), & Whedon, J. (Story). (1997). School Hard (Season 2, Episode 3) [TV series episode]. In *Buffy the Vampire Slayer*. Mutant Enemy Productions; 20th Century Fox Television.

8. Singelis, T. M. (1994). The measurement of independent and interdependent self-construals. *Personality and Social Psychology Bulletin*, 20(5), 580–591.

9. Humphrey, R. H. (2013). *Effective leadership: Theory, cases, and applications.* Sage Publications.

10. Petrie, D. (Writer), & Marck, N. (Director). (2000). Fool for Love (Season 5, Episode 7) [TV series episode]. In *Buffy the Vampire Slayer*. Mutant Enemy Productions; 20th Century Fox Television.

11. Sluss, D. M., & Ashforth, B. E. (2007). Relational identity and identification: Defining ourselves through work relationships. *Academy of Management Review*, 32(1), 9–32.

12. Smith, H. J., Tyler, T. R., & Huo, Y. J. (2003). Interpersonal treatment, social identity, and organizational behavior. *Social identity at work: Developing theory for organizational practice*, 155–171.

13. Hogg, M. A., & Williams, K. D. (2000). From I to we: Social identity and the collective self. *Group dynamics: Theory, research, and practice*, 4(1), 81.

14. Van Stekelenburg, J. (2013). Collective identity. In D. Snow, D. Della Porta, B. Klandermans, & D. McAdam (Eds.), *The Wiley-Blackwell encyclopedia of social and political movements* (pp. 219–225). Wiley-Blackwell.

15. Thomas, E. F., Mavor, K. I., & McGarty, C. (2012). Social identities facilitate and encapsulate action-relevant constructs: A test of the social identity model of collective action. *Group Processes & Intergroup Relations*, 15(1), 75–88.

16. Espenson, J. (Writer), & Contner, J. A. (Director). (1999). The Harsh Light of Day (Season 4, Episode 2) [TV series episode]. In *Buffy the Vampire Slayer*. Mutant Enemy Productions; 20th Century Fox Television.

8

RESILIENCE (OR HOW TO PREVENT GETTING STAKED INTO DUST PERMANENTLY)

Here, we come swooping in at number eight, chapter wise, and let me say that, at this point, we're getting closer to the end than we are to the beginning. Resilience is a quality that one reads about and learns about a lot, and indeed, there are a plethora of terms to use to describe resilience. There's grit of course, and tenacity too, but I would hazard a guess that the most popular term for this quality is resilience. One could be permitted to even speculate that among this trio of words, the most resilient word is resilience. It sounds just right – to use a Goldilocks and the three bears type of metaphor, the word is mot juste.

Resilience of course refers to the ability to bounce back from failure or adversity of some sort. There are times of course when it is perhaps better to fail or walk away from the failure than to constantly keep being resilient, but by and large, resilience is a good quality for anyone including leaders to possess. And in BtVS, we get loads of characters, both heroic and villainous, who demonstrate and display excellent resilience. Honestly, I can probably name everyone in the Scooby Gang or even among the villains and have an example of a situation or incident of them displaying resilience.

In this chapter, I will first start us off by discussing the definition and description of resilience, especially in terms of how it relates to and matters in leadership. Next, I will present several examples from BtVS that highlight resilience, so be tenacious, and read through them, as I really do think they will improve overall comprehension of the topic. After that, I will discuss the circumstances when one shouldn't be forcing oneself to continue being resilient – after all, resilience shouldn't be this bottomless pit that one keeps on displaying. At a certain point, it behooves a person to quit being resilient just for the sake of resilience. I will discuss how one can figure out when that point arrives. Finally, I will discuss ways by which individuals can improve their own resilience ability. And as always, I will use many examples of characters and situations from BtVS. So, let's get to the somewhat formalish definition of resilience next.

RESILIENCE, TENACITY, GRIT, PERSEVERANCE, ET AL.

As I mentioned earlier, resilience has so many terms associated with it that one could get away by calling it any of those terms. I am sticking to the resilience word because as per me, it captures the essence of the quality in a perfect way. So, what is the formal definition of the term then? Here's a somewhat Gilesian way of writing it – it can be defined as one's ability to regain balance following an exposure to adverse events.[1-3] At this point, many a reader will probably purse their lips and say, "Bloody Hell" in a manner reminiscent of an increasingly irate Spike. But then again, unless you love complex definitions, I would imagine that you would prefer a simpler definition. So, let's just say that resilience is the ability of an individual to face failure, and be able to come back and try again, instead of giving up without any fuss. Basically, an individual with resilience perseveres until they finally get what they strove to. Oh, and that's another word that often is used in a resilience context: perseverance.

While the above will prove to be quite interesting for a wordsmith, the reality is that all of those terms are roughly for the same construct. At this point, I must mention that in the academic literature[4-7] (some disciplines chiefly in education), grit is considered slightly different from resilience, which is considered slightly different from perseverance, etc. In the literature on psychology and business though, resilience is considered a major component of psychological capital[8-11] (which also includes hope, optimism, and confidence). All four components together make up one's psychological capital profile. I suppose, I am veering toward the Luthans approach to resilience in this chapter though as opposed to the more education-based approach. I will be focused on resilience, and resilience alone, out of these four components of psychological capital. Well, primarily because to me, it's the most malleable quantity of the four. Confidence can be built sure, and one can perhaps learn to become more hopeful and optimistic (a tall order for some people though, I can tell you). But resilience is something that is a lot more actionable and fairly straightforward to build one's levels up.

However, to avoid getting bogged down in an overly academic discussion that wouldn't be out of place in a Watcher's Council meeting, I will be using and referring to only resilience in this chapter. After all, call a vampire a vampyr or a vrykolakas or a strigoi, the meaning is roughly the same. Anyhow, let's get to discussing some examples from BtVS that exemplify resilience.

WHO EXEMPLIFIES RESILIENCE?

One of the saddest episodes in the entire series is the one where Joyce, Buffy (and Dawn's) mother suddenly dies. A real shocker, that episode,[12] and we viscerally see how Buffy falls apart in the beginning. It's very realistic and anyone who's suffered the loss of a beloved parent or a parental figure can empathize with Buffy (and Dawn) in this situation. Right off the bat, when she discovers Joyce's lifeless body, Buffy practically goes paralytic with shock. She registers complete denial of the harsh fact that her mother has passed, yet she still knows to call 911. And even after the emergency paramedics come, Buffy continues to exhibit a totally numb countenance.

Indeed, for all purposes, it appeared as though her grief has gotten the best of her. However, despite the shock of the moment, Buffy rebounds from it, after going through the various stages of grief, and emerges again as the Slayer, and the protector of her sister. One could almost argue that the presence of Dawn helped Buffy avoid totally breaking down with grief, and indeed, one could credit Dawn with helping Buffy remain resilient. Indeed, I would state here that this episode more than any other truly shows Buffy at her most resilient. You can only demonstrate your resilience when you push yourself to keep going on despite maybe wanting to just curl up into a ball of nothingness. And Buffy does that in ample amounts, by struggling through, and yes, relying on her friends and well-wishers, but buckling up to ensure that she continues to protect Dawn and others as the Slayer. This is of course, just one example of a time when Buffy demonstrated tremendous resilience, but nevertheless, it is an example that I really think shows Buffy's resilience with the utmost clarity.

Another character from the BtVS world that really exemplified resilience is Xander. I've written in other chapters about how Xander's superpower is his ability to notice things and be there for his friends as a dependable friend (leaving aside the time when he stood up Anya on the evening of the wedding), but the fact that truly captures his resilience is that Xander among all the Scoobies probably has the worst family circumstances of all (not just emotionally unavailable like Willow's but sort of physically abusive too). While it is true that Buffy has an absent father, she at least has a loving mother and sister. Xander, on the other hand, has a visibly dysfunctional family (who started fighting with Anya's side of the family during the wedding over petty matters), which is how Stewart Burns the demon[13] was even able to psychologically prime Xander into walking out on his future bride on the day of the wedding.

Despite all of the baggage that Xander indubitably had in his life, thanks to his dysfunctional and abusive family circumstances, Xander still somehow found the ability in himself to be one of the most dependable and joyful members of the Scooby Gang. His brand of resilience demonstrates that people do not have to let their rough familial circumstances dictate their own personality or values. If anything, Xander was doubly determined to not repeat any of the mistakes committed by his parents and family, and as I've repeatedly mentioned, this went as far as him walking out on Anya on the day of the wedding because he was terrified of repeating the mistakes he saw his parents make during their marriage. Yes, one could argue that Xander wasn't truly showing resilience here, but he really was in an oblique sort of way. The main thing preying on his mind was his refusal to subject Anya to an unhappy life similar to the one experienced by his parents.

Staying with the core Scooby Group, let's discuss Willow Rosenberg next in a resilience context. Unlike Xander, Willow had a fairly banal familial experience, even if her parents were emotionally unavailable to her. Willow truly developed community and kinship through the Scooby Gang, but one could argue that she truly blossomed into a person wholly accepting of herself in college when she first met and then became close with Tara (this was after they both discovered that the Daughters of Gaea was a rather disappointing group of non-witches just pretending to spell cast). Willow first discovered her penchant for magic during the time when she was trying to re-ensoul Angelus and thus turn him back into Angel (the Battle around Acathla's dimension). And one can see how Willow plods on while learning and absorbing magic like a sponge. Indeed, without Willow's resilience and magical prowess guiding them, they never would have been able to resurrect Buffy.

Yes, she does end up getting addicted to the allure of magic and that eventually leads to the entire Dark Willow episode. But even there after the events that finally culminate in Dark Willow retreating and lovable Willow eventually returning to the fold, one can see the resilience with which Willow bounces back. When she's with Giles in Westbury, England, learning meditation and magic with a coven of English Wiccans in order to rehabilitate Willow. The rehabilitation was necessary since Willow was suffering a lot of guilt and regret after having killed Warren in such a brutal fashion, as well as hurting her closest and dearest friends, who were akin to family for her. If she had lacked resilience at this stage, then it is doubtful that her rehabilitation would have been successful.

Another character I would like to write about here is Faith Lehane, the bad girl Slayer to Buffy's good girl Slayer. In the early days of the series, she's introduced as a deeply flawed Slayer, who is a good person but is hinted to be more of a loose cannon, and with a dark side to her. Then she really does go fully dark when she joins up with the evil Mayor Wilkins in his plot to ascend to a demon form to gain more power and be immortal. But through it all, no matter if she was playing for the right team or the wrong team, Faith retains a stunning sense of resilience, at times, probably even more resilient than Buffy. But of course, she also has her moments when it looks like her resilience is failing, but she usually manages to pull through and be resilient again.

Returning to the familial environment, both of Faith's parents were said to be alcoholics, who didn't exactly provide her with a stable and loving home atmosphere. Despite their somewhat insalubrious parenting style, Faith still managed to go on to become a Slayer herself. One also sees Faith's resilience vis-à-vis Kakistos.[14] That cloven-footed traditionalist (funny that his traditionalist outlook eventually cost him the services of Mr. Trick) vampire had killed Faith's original Watcher, and continued to stalk and pursue Faith, even as far as Sunnydale. During the final fight between Kakistos and the two Slayers, Faith seems like she's losing her sense of composure and almost falling apart, when Buffy's yelling to her to not die jolts her back to reality, and Faith finally dusts Kakistos, in a stunning display of resilience (this is especially satisfying to watch because Kakistos had brutally killed Faith's Watcher).

As the above examples of resilience show, each person's resilience was tested by a different adverse situation. For Buffy, it had to do with the loss of a parent, and for Willow, it had to do with overcoming regret and guilt. For Xander, it had to do with avoiding what he thought was a certain unpleasant outcome, and for Faith, it had to do with getting a difficult task accomplished. All very different yet adverse situations, but they all required resilience to get accomplished. Without resilience, it is possible all these individuals would have succumbed to the adverse situations.

Now that I have discussed at length what resilience is, and provided examples of BtvS characters displaying resilience, it is time to move to another topic which I want to do a bit of expounding on, namely, when do you stop being overly resilient? Sometimes, it just isn't worth the effort to be resilient in certain matters, but how does a person know when that point is?

DON'T BECOME OVER-RESILIENT

As discussed previously, resilience is an excellent quality for an individual to possess, and it is especially important for a leader because leaders are often facing precarious situations for their organizations. But like everything out there, there can be times when one needs to cut out being resilient and just eat the loss. In some ways, it's like escalation of commitment. The individual engaging in that probably thinks everyone sees him or her as a super resilient person and cheers them on. That may be true in the beginning, but eventually after a string of failures, the cheering fades considerably. I know an individual who's been trying to clear an exam for the better part of a dozen years, and they have not succeeded once during these dozen years. It's basically a case of keep preparing for 11 months, and then taking the exam, and then back to square one, once the attempt is unsuccessful. To me this is a clear case of where it is high time to give up on that particular goal.

See the aftermath of this sort of resilience for that individual – it's 12 years without having a fulltime job and subsequently 12 years of lost earnings and skill deterioration. I mean, why try for the 13th time now, it's not like anyone ever says "The thirteenth time will be lucky." I would have suggested quitting the game right after the 5th or 6th attempt and moving on to some other career choice. This individual is way too steeped in the sunk cost fallacy, which is where you end up thinking that because you've invested so much time and resources into something, you have to keep trying to accomplish that.

Similarly, there are leaders who display their resilience by pursuing a goal doggedly and with great determination. Despite market failure or a lack of enthusiasm by clients or employees, they persist and insist that the plan or strategy will finally work and bear fruit. That is clearly a case of escalation of commitment, that is, when you feel that you have put in too much time and effort already into an action, that pulling out will be wasteful, so you keep on doing it in the vain hope that it will finally become successful. There are so many examples of leaders and CEOs who have done precisely that and thereby steered their countries or companies straight into the deepest gutter. Think about historical leaders who pursued war against other kingdoms, and suffered losses, just because they failed to consider that their strategies needed to change.

You can see this happening in BtVS as well where individuals took certain actions despite the sacrifice involved and chose not to pursue resilience. Consider Oz for instance – he and Willow had a great thing going, but his werewolf nature threatened to go out of hand. Even though he was careful about taking precautions, all of that went out the window when he was confronted by Veruca, another werewolf like him. That led to a situation where he ended up cheating on Willow with Veruca, and it hurt Willow, and led to their breakup. This might seem counterintuitive because from all accounts Willow seemed to be willing to give them another chance, but Oz was the one who initiated the breakup, because he really did not trust himself to be able to withstand his werewolf urges.[15]

He chose to leave Sunnydale instead, and while he does come back (and gets super jealous of her closeness with Tara), he ends up getting captured by the initiative and is finally rescued by Buffy and Riley. But his decision to leave in the first place can be seen as an excellent way to avoid escalation of commitment. Think about it – if Oz had continued to stay on, it is doubtless that the wolf in him would have arisen again at some or the other point, so it made more sense for him to leave the relationship and town. Even though they had a great relationship barring that one Veruca episode, Oz knew that despite all that they had shared and the time they had spent together, the next time the wolf came out, it could be harmful for Willow.

So, in a sense, Oz decided to call it off in order to prevent any other werewolf incidents in the future. He also knew that trust once gone (thanks to his having cheated on her) can never be brought back to the heights it once used to occupy. So, his decision to leave and break it off with Willow can be seen as a way to prevent escalation of commitment. Yes, it may appear that Oz wasn't being resilient in that context, but it was a lot better for him to walk away early rather than wait for something worse to happen due to his inability to control his lupine instincts. When it comes to leaders and most individuals too, they have got to be able to figure out the point where their resilience might be getting to be too much. If it's failure after failure after failure, then it's time to reinvest your time in something else. Really no benefit in flogging the dead horse, as it isn't going to suddenly charge up and win the race. Keep an eye out, and if it looks like your efforts are simply not working out, then pivot away from that course of action and avoid getting trapped in a bog of escalation of commitment. I will now discuss how leaders can improve their own resilience.

A FOOLPROOF WAY TO IMPROVE RESILIENCE

Honestly, there's no other real way to improve resilience than to train oneself to be able to face adversity. If you're in law enforcement, then you had better focus on your physical fitness and ability to recognize patterns in criminal behavior. Train for it, as Giles would suggest. If you recall, Giles was a pretty stern taskmaster when it came to training. He was quite insistent that Buffy spend a lot of time in training with him and also staying active in terms of patrolling for vampires. In some ways, Giles seems a bit surprised that Buffy also has desires to do normal girl things besides training and sparring and tactical training. But honestly, without Giles' approach to training, it is likely that Buffy may have easily lost to some vampires and possibly have gotten killed early on. Thanks to Giles' insistence on keeping the training going, Buffy basically built up her reservoir of resilience and was able to tackle most adverse situations with aplomb.

So, just like Buffy, you too need to train yourself in whatever arena you're working in. If you happen to be in chemistry, make sure to keep up on the latest developments in chemistry, or if you're in athletics, keep training and improving yourself. The day you stop training, your skills are going to become rusty, and it'll be that much harder to go back into action or be able to bounce back if you happen to suffer a failure. Just be sure though to not end up in a situation of over-resilience where you're just continually doing the same thing without actually doing anything useful.

Another way to improve one's sense of resilience is to build up backup plans and conjure up different contingencies. After all, everything isn't going to be amazing all the time, and there are definitely times when it'll feel like the Hellmouth just erupted, so may as well be proactive and plan ahead. Tactical training as Giles would put it – it's an important skill in a leader's toolkit. These two ways can really build up one's resilience level, so I would encourage everyone to work on these two elements in order to build up their resilience levels. Just be careful not to get too steeped in resilience that you forget that at times you've simply got to disengage to protect yourself or the ones you love. Be resilient but don't become entangled in over-resilience; you've got to be able to disengage when the situation demands.

SUMMARY

This chapter discussed resilience and discussed what exactly resilience is. I also discussed the differences in conceptualizing resilience and other related terms such as perseverance, tenacity, and grit. I list and describe several examples of BtVS characters as they demonstrate resilience in their unique adverse circumstances. Following that, I next discuss escalation of commitment in terms of over-resilience and discuss how one is to avoid getting into that sort of situation. I essentially state that in times like that, it may be better to exit rather than to continue being resilient. After all, you really don't want to be staked into a pile of dust, but neither do you want to keep repeating unsuccessful ideas out of a misplaced idea of resilience.

Finally, I discuss two ways by which someone can improve their own resilience levels. In the next chapter, I will discuss the themes of revenge and redemption in leadership, which is particularly pertinent in today's global climate. And of course, BtVS is absolutely chockful of both revenge and redemption from start to finish, so let's finally finish this chapter and move on the start of the next.

REFERENCES

1. Linnenluecke, M. K. (2017). Resilience in business and management research: A review of influential publications and a research agenda. *International Journal of Management Reviews*, *19*(1), 4–30.

2. Ayala, J. C., & Manzano, G. (2014). The resilience of the entrepreneur. Influence on the success of the business. A longitudinal analysis. *Journal of Economic Psychology*, *42*, 126–135.

3. Eliot, J. L. (2020). Resilient leadership: The impact of a servant leader on the resilience of their followers. *Advances in Developing Human Resources*, *22*(4), 404–418.

4. Datu, J. A. D. (2021). Beyond passion and perseverance: Review and future research initiatives on the science of grit. *Frontiers in Psychology*, *11*, 545526.

5. Caporale-Berkowitz, N. A., Boyer, B. P., Muenks, K., & Brownson, C. B. (2022). Resilience, not grit, predicts college student retention following academic probation. *Journal of Educational Psychology*, *114*(7), 1654.

6. Caza, A., Caza, B. B., & Baloochi, M. E. (2020). Resilient personality: Is grit a source of resilience? In E. Powley, B. B. Caza, & A. Caza (Eds.), *Research handbook on organizational resilience* (pp. 25–38). Edward Elgar Publishing.

7. Georgoulas-Sherry, V., & Kelly, D. (2019). Resilience, grit, and hardiness: Determining the relationships amongst these constructs through structural equation modeling techniques. *Journal of Positive Psychology and Wellbeing*, *3*(2), 165–178.

8. Luthans, F., & Youssef-Morgan, C. M. (2017). Psychological capital: An evidence-based positive approach. *Annual Review of Organizational Psychology and Organizational Behavior*, *4*(1), 339–366.

9. Luthans, F., Vogelgesang, G. R., & Lester, P. B. (2006). Developing the psychological capital of resiliency. *Human Resource Development Review*, *5*(1), 25–44.

10. Luthans, F., Youssef, C. M., & Avolio, B. J. (2006). *Psychological capital: Developing the human competitive edge*. Oxford University Press.

11. Gooty, J., Gavin, M., Johnson, P. D., Frazier, M. L., & Snow, D. B. (2009). In the eyes of the beholder: Transformational leadership, positive psychological capital, and performance. *Journal of Leadership & Organizational Studies*, *15*(4), 353–367.

12. Whedon, J. (Writer & Director). (2001). The body (Season 5, Episode 16) [TV episode]. In *Buffy the Vampire Slayer*. Mutant Enemy Productions.

13. Kirschner, R. (Writer), & Solomon, D. (Director). (2002). Hell's bells (Season 6, Episode 16) [TV episode]. In *Buffy the Vampire Slayer*. Mutant Enemy Productions.

14. Greenwalt, D. (Writer), & Contner, J. A. (Director). (1998). Faith, hope & trick (Season 3, Episode 1) [TV series episode]. In *Buffy the Vampire Slayer*. Mutant Enemy Productions; 20th Century Fox Television.

15. Noxon, M. (Writer), & Grossman, D. (Director). (1999). Wild at heart (Season 4, Episode 6) [TV series episode]. In *Buffy the Vampire Slayer*. Mutant Enemy Productions; 20th Century Fox Television.

9

REVENGE VERSUS REDEMPTION – A NAY OR ANYA?

Revenge and redemption are two words you often see in tandem, in popular culture or in regular life too, come to think of it. In the BtVS world, you see a lot of it. So many characters motivated by revenge, and so many motivated by a sense of redemption, and many a time, the same character might engage in both sets of behaviors. It may seem odd to see these themes in a book about leadership, but the reason I am bringing in this somewhat unorthodox theme into this book is that I believe both revenge and redemption are very much situated and present in a leadership context.

They are both definitely present in ample quantities in BtVS. Think about Angel – the whole reason he even existed as Angel is because he got cursed by the Kalderash people into having his soul back.[1] Next, think about Principal Woods[2] – he was also consumed with the idea of obtaining revenge for the killing of his mother by Spike. And of course, as the title of this chapter may hint, one can hardly forget Anya or Anyanka can one, she of the quintessential revenge demon variety. And then speaking of redemption in particular, Andrew Wells of the supremely irksome Trio also got an excellent redemption arc. There are others too, and I will talk about their redemption and revenge journeys in the chapter.

In this chapter, I will first discuss what exactly revenge and redemption are. Next, I will discuss how revenge and redemption truly apply in a leadership context, and what exactly a leader can do in terms of handling their own or other people's desire for revenge, or desire for redemption. As always, I will illustrate and illuminate on these topics by providing several examples and instances of characters from BtVS who either stuck to a path of revenge or got on to the path of redemption, or indeed, even traversed either of the two paths while straddling the other. So, let's start off with discussing what exactly revenge and redemption are about.

R IS FOR REVENGE

Let's start off with revenge first. Revenge is basically a personal response to injustice or unjust treatment.[3-7] Essentially, a person thinks of or acts to correct the injustice he or she has suffered. They may never act on it, but they sure think about it. The injustice that they suffer or experience is drastic enough to want them to take revenge. In BtVS, we see plenty of characters all in various stages of revenge seeking. On the one hand, we have vengeance demons whose existence is to allow revenge seekers the recourse to take revenge on those that have wronged them. D'Hoffryn and his other vengeance demons have a thriving line of work throughout the entire BtVS series.

From a general leader perspective too, you might find situations where leaders themselves have desires to engage in acts of revenge. We see this a lot in politics especially, where politicians of different stripes and flavors often exact revenge from their rival politicians. Cases and allegations are leveled at each other, and in some countries, it goes as far as bloody murder with assassinations being plotted.[8-10] You also see this happening in a regular business context, where business leaders take revenge on their rivals, for some perceived injustice. In some cases, there may not actually be any injustice perpetrated, but injustice is somewhat in the eye of the beholder, so there is individual-level variance in whether or not an act of revenge is actually genuinely merited or not.

From a BtVS perspective, think about the curse that the Kalderash people put on Angelus.[1] The curse was their way of getting revenge on Angelus, who had killed one of the tribe's elder's daughters. As a result, they put an ensoulment curse on Angelus to make him feel regret and torment for the many atrocities he had committed as a vampire. However, that revenge didn't just end with the ensoulment of Angelus – instead, Darla, Spike, and Drusilla laid waste to the entire encampment of the Kalderash people. That also was an act of revenge, so as you can see, revenge begets revenge in that case. Of course, it also results in Angelus starting his transformation into Angel, as he's unable to kill the baby that Darla wants him to kill to prove to her that he's still vampirish enough despite having a soul. But there's no denying that revenge was the primary mover of all these occurrences. And revenge does have consequences, some expected and others entirely unexpected.

Another example of revenge from the BtVS world centers on our favorite vengeance demon turned human turned demon turned human again Anya/Anyanka. As I've mentioned before in this book, she was Aud earlier, and then furious at her partner Olaf's cheating on her, she concocts revenge on him through a spell and converts him into a troll. This attracts the attention of D'Hoffryn, who is impressed and offers her a transformation into Anyanka, the patron saint (still a demon though) of scorned women, accompanied by a magical pendant. We see her come into the timeline of the Scooby Gang when she first appears due to Cordelia's anguish at seeing Xander kiss Willow. This of course leads to a situation where Cordelia's wish that Buffy never comes to Sunnydale creates a dismal alternative future for the town. Giles does eventually figure out to break the pendant and thus render Anyanka powerless and a normal human being again.

Now let's switch gears to a leadership context. In our decidedly non-magical and non-hellmouth afflicted world, we still get to see a lot of revenge in the workplace. This revenge can be bi-directional or unidirectional, or multi-directional even. One of the reasons why an atmosphere of revenge even exists in a workplace is due to a miscarriage of organizational justice. There are multiple forms of organizational justice – you've got distributive justice, procedural justice, interactional justice, and restorative justice.[11-15] Distributive justice has to do with the fairness of allocation of resources, while procedural justice has to do with the fairness of processes. Interactional justice has to do with how respectful the interactions between leaders and followers are, and restorative justice has to do with repairing harm to the victim of the injustice. A transgression which contravenes any of these justice forms can trigger a desire for revenge. If as a leader, your organization is replete with instances of injustice, be they any of the above four forms, there will be acts of revenge that will happen. Sometimes, the leaders themselves may be at the receiving end of revenge, or they might be the ones meting it out, and either situation is not exactly a desirable state of affairs.

Research has shown that revenge tends to keep sparking further acts of revenge, which ultimately benefits nobody. In particular, peace studies research (a discipline which focuses on peace) finds that revenge can spark conflict, which can then lead to a prolonged period of violence. And even from an organizational perspective, revenge and retribution are likely to keep happening, unless there are concrete steps taken to usher in sustainable peace. So, this is what I would propose based off of what research has to offer us. One form of justice which is particularly insidious in terms of having harmful consequences if not adhered to is interactional justice. The kind where interactions between people are assessed for fairness and dignity in that if each person is being treated with dignity in the interaction. If this form of justice is low, then you can bet there'll be an atmosphere ripe for revenge acts to occur.

One way for the leader to try to stave off acts of revenge before they even begin is to focus on interactional justice. Ensuring an atmosphere of respect and fairness will go a long way to ensuring that there will be no scope for revenge or retribution acts. Well, it might mean lean times for D'Hoffryn's band of vengeance demons, but at least the organizations and the people within them will be delighted at the interactional justice prevalent there. And of course, if there should be a breach of injustice, leaders should do their best to try to at least resolve it with restorative justice. Out of the four forms of justice, as per me, the restorative justice form is perhaps the hardest kind to accomplish, because in some cases, there might not be anything you can do to restore the situation to pre-injustice times, and whatever you do try, could potentially create further injustice.

To elaborate on that last point – consider the events in the third season of BtVS, on the *Gingerbread*[16] episode. This is the episode where Joyce and Sheila are very involved in the Mothers Opposed to the Occult (MOO) group, and under the influence of the demon who appears periodically every 50 years to convince people to kill witches. The MOO group was organized supposedly to bring about restorative justice, but it sure quickly deteriorates into a lynch mob where the group and other people associated with it become as bloodthirsty as the demon who's brainwashed them into doing things their ordinary selves would never dream of. In a sense, that attempt at restorative justice quickly veered off into an episode of unbridled vigilantism. There is another form of justice, which is called vigilante justice.

In vigilante justice,[17,18] the whole point is to correct injustice using vigilante tools. So, as you can imagine, vigilante justice could involve some drastic measures at times. People basically believe that the process is completely unfair, and so they go outside of the process to usher in justice. But as we saw with the events in *Gingerbread*, vigilantism sometimes causes innocent people to suffer along with the guilty parties. So, it is a form of justice that is equally hard to implement because of the risk of unintended consequences. And an atmosphere where revenge keeps spreading is ripe for unintended consequences. So, I would suggest that leaders try and reduce the revenge factor potential in their organizations, and the best way to do that is to focus on procedural and interactional justice. Those are fairly straightforward and easily doable steps. Now let's shift gears and move along to the redemption side of things.

R IS FOR REDEMPTION

Both revenge and redemption could be likened to being the faces of a Janus sculpture of sorts.[19-20] For those a bit rusty on their Roman history, Janus was basically a god with two faces, one face looking forward, and the other looking backward 9. In a way, you could cast revenge and redemption as one of these two faces of Janus, with redemption usually being the forward-facing face, and revenge the backward facing face (I mean there are probably situations when the situation could be reversed, but ceteris paribus, revenge is backward facing while redemption is forward facing).

Redemption can be defined in a variety of ways (like most concepts and constructs can), but the one that fits our narrative best is the one relating it to the act of saving or being saved from evil. Essentially, redemption is tied in with forgiveness and moral goodness. We have loads of redemption arcs in BtVS. The most famous ones revolve around Angel and Spike, but I want to focus a bit more on Anyanka/Anya here. After all, the chapter is named after her, so to avoid false advertising, I do need to feature her prominently here. I've written a little bit about Anya previously in the book and alluded to the fact that she was a vengeance demon who turns into a human and then becomes a vengeance demon again and is again turned into a human. It's a real cyclical pattern there for her, as she weaves in between a revenge state and a redemption state.

But overall, I think Anya had a real redemption arc, because in the end, she is on the side of the protagonists, during the battle against the First Evil. And in fact, her redemption is also instrumental in the redemption of another character, namely, Andrew Wells. Both the characters weave into revenge/

redemption modes rather seamlessly. But Anya in particular has a very interesting and real redemption arc. Think about individuals who are in real life trying to redeem themselves (e.g., a person who just served time in prison and is trying to rehabilitate their image). Their road to redemption isn't a straight and smooth one, but instead is quite bumpy in patches, and with plenty of hurdles to pass as well. Anyanka/Anya certainly had a very bumpy road in her road to redemption. After thousands of years of existence as a demon, it is inevitable that her history as a demon would continue to influence her human self. But indubitably, Anya tried really hard to fit in. While she never did master the fine art of polite verbal communication, she was well-intentioned for the most part especially after falling in love with Xander.

Her road to redemption was bumpy but was steady and only took a drastic stop after the fiasco around the broken off marriage with Xander. That caused her to resume her vengeance demon avatar, and she starts to grant wishes to spurned women again. One time, Anya grants a wish to a girl (Rachel) that ends up in a Grimslaw demon[21] (a large spider-like demon) killing several fraternity boys in college. Rachel's wish was that the frat boys ought to experience the pain of having their hearts torn out, and that's literally what happened thanks to the Grimslaw demon. This is what puts her face to face in battle with Buffy and Willow, and it's a no-holds barred kind of fight, but eventually, Anya's full turn into being an evil vengeance demon is prevented by her empathy, which she seems to have inculcated from her time as a human with the Scooby Gang and her relationship with Xander specifically. She asks D'Hoffryn to take back the wish she's granted, and he does, but also strips her powers away, and kills her best friend Halfrek in the process. So, that redemption does come with consequences; in her quest for revenge, somewhat obliquely directed at Xander, she ends up not being able to go through with it because she still retains an element of love toward Xander.

Later on, in the BtVS seventh season, Anya actually strikes up a pretty good relationship with Andrew. This is probably due to three main reasons – both have experienced being the villains prior to being on the good side, and as a result, neither one of them were fully trusted by the Scoobies or by the potential Slayers. Additionally, Andrew's awkward but good-natured way of communication really was the polar opposite of Anya's blunter way of speaking. Also, later, when Andrew kind of casts himself as the Scooby's unofficially official raconteur, he and Anya got along even better. In some ways, their growing friendship almost has a sibling like quality to it. In the end, this Anya–Andrew friendship really does help in rehabilitating Andrew's image with the Scoobys, and he is almost considered a semi-pseudo member of the Scooby Gang. Later on, in the follow-up comics, Andrew get more opportunities to help the Scooby Gang, but as far as the BtVS television show is concerned (and we're only focusing on the show in this book), Andrew's redemption arc gets completed during season 7 and in part due to his friendship with Anya (who has her own redemption arc going on in season 7).

Another thing to note here is that Andrew essentially gets co-opted into the Scooby Gang in a gradual sort of way. In the beginning, he's picked up by the Scoobies as a hostage, partly to keep him safe from the First Evil but also partly to keep him out of trouble. These events happened after Andrew had already killed Jonathan with the Dagger of Lex. He did so because he was under the influence of the First Evil, which promised him that the original Trio would live on as gods. So, the Scoobies' decision to capture Andrew was a smart one because they couldn't trust him to be out and about doing the First Evil's bidding, whether under duress or not. Eventually, during this capture, the Scoobies got to begrudgingly trust him a bit more every day even though they never quite trusted him completely (at least not on the show). But his redemption was slow and steady, not quick and bumpy like Anya's. Now, let's head on to another section that talks about what leaders ought to do vis-à-vis this Janus-faced concept of revenge and redemption.

WHAT SHOULD LEADERS DO ABOUT THESE 2 RS?

Essentially, what leaders need to do about revenge and redemption is to understand that no-matter what kind of organization they lead, there is going to be a potential act of revenge or an opportunity for redemption present in that organization. That is a rather fastidious task for any leader to consider because it involves being rather a fine-tuner. A veritable magician of sorts. Because, on the one hand, you have to try to make sure that the climate or culture in your organization is one that doesn't allow a revenge culture to spread.

So basically, you have to ensure that all forms of organizational justice types are adhered to – distributive, procedural, interactional, and should any not be then you have to ensure that restorative justice is at least applied to the situation of injustice. And if it so happens that you find that there's a systemic issue in your workplace be it between the managers and the managed, you've got to step in and resolve it. While it is fairly straightforward, it can still be complex. After all, sometimes, the most straightforward tasks can still have a high degree of intricacy involved.

About redemption, it's more tied in with restorative justice of a sort. If someone commits a mistake, and is truly repentant about it, and there's a need or desire to rehabilitate that person, then of course, redemption is a good choice to offer to the person. I do realize that there are certain crimes or transgressions that are simply not candidates for rehabilitation based on how severe they are. But generally speaking, if the transgression isn't too severe, and the transgressor has a desire to improve, then it might be a good idea for the leader to help in the redemption process.

Both these goals can be accomplished if the leader establishes a culture or climate that is conducive for allowing organizational justice to flourish in the organization if there is an element of forgiveness inbuilt into the company culture. Without an element of forgiveness, there can be no redemption. Consider the Scooby Gang for instance – while they never did completely trust Andrew in the beginning, they eventually grew to trust him somewhat. The same applied for Anya too – there was an element of distrust toward her, but that eventually passed, and the Scooby Gang accepted her as a bona fide member. The same can be said to be true for both Angel and Spike, who were both semi-included in the Scooby Gang. In all these cases, it's due to Buffy's willingness to give a bit of trust in those individuals seeking out their own redemption. Remember, in comparison to Buffy, Giles wasn't all that forgiving toward transgressors and past-villains.

So, straightforward, but complex to run in most organizations. It does require a two-pronged approach; on the one hand, a willingness to forgive and allow for redemption, and the other to correct or prevent any sort of injustice. Only that will ensure that the company will be poised to allow for either prevention or amelioration of injustice, as well as allow repentant transgressors the option of redeeming themselves. Without having the option of redemption, revenge may become a limitless circle. Leaders need to be prepared to stop such endless circles as they are not conducive to anything. One certainly does not want a recreation of a Wishverse or Bizarro Land[22] (as famously termed by Cordelia Chase) in one's organization and that's exactly what a place with endless revenge cycles will become like.

SUMMARY

In this chapter, I discussed the concepts of revenge and redemption and discussed how we can trace their origins from an organizational justice/injustice perspective. I discuss several characters from BtVS who help illustrate the concepts of revenge and redemption and also discuss how leaders can use this information to help prevent their organizations from turning into cesspools of endless revenge cycles. In the next chapter, we will follow through with a solid discussion of followership. So please do follow along, and see you in Chapter 10.

REFERENCES

1. Whedon, J. (Writer & Director). (1998). Becoming, Part 1 (Season 2, Episode 21) [TV episode]. In *Buffy the Vampire Slayer*. Mutant Enemy Productions.

2. Fury, D., & Goddard, D. (Writers), & Fury, D. (Director). (2003). Lies My Parents Told Me (Season 7, Episode 17) [TV series episode]. In *Buffy the Vampire Slayer*. Mutant Enemy Productions; 20th Century Fox Television.

3. Bies, R. J., & Tripp, T. M. (2005). The study of revenge in the workplace: Conceptual, ideological, and empirical issues. In S. Fox & P. E. Spector (Eds.), *Counterproductive work behavior: Investigations of actors and targets* (pp. 65–81). American Psychological Association. https://doi.org/10.1037/10893-003

4. Tripp, T. M., & Bies, R. J. (2010). "Righteous" anger and revenge in the workplace: The fantasies, the feuds, the forgiveness. In M. Potegal, G. Stemmler, & C. Spielberger (Eds.), *International handbook of anger: Constituent and concomitant biological, psychological, and social processes* (pp. 413–431). Springer. https://doi.org/10.1007/978-0-387-89676-2_24

5. Tripp, T. M., Bies, R. J., & Aquino, K. (2002). Poetic justice or petty jealousy? The aesthetics of revenge. *Organizational behavior and human decision processes*, 89(1), 966–984.

6. Tripp, T. M., & Bies, R. J. (2009). *Getting even: The truth about workplace revenge–and how to stop it*. John Wiley & Sons.

7. Tripp, T. M., & Bies, J. (2015). "Doing justice": The role of motives for revenge in the workplace. In R. Cropanzano & M. L. Ambrose (Eds.), *The Oxford handbook of justice in the workplace* (pp. 461–475). Oxford University Press.

8. Ben-Yehuda, N. (1997). Political assassination events as a cross-cultural form of alternative justice. *International Journal of Comparative Sociology*, 38(1–2), 25–47.

9. Löwenheim, O., & Heimann, G. (2008). Revenge in international politics. *Security Studies, 17*(4), 685–724.

10. Bell, J. B. (2017). *Assassin: Theory and practice of political violence.* Routledge.

11. Colquitt, J. A., Greenberg, J., & Zapata-Phelan, C. P. (2012). Organizational justice. *The Oxford Handbook of Organizational Psychology, 1,* 526–547.

12. Greenberg, J. (1990). Organizational justice: Yesterday, today, and tomorrow. *Journal of Management, 16*(2), 399–432.

13. Colquitt, J., Greenberg, J., & Zapata-Phelan, C. (2005). What is organizational justice? A historical overview. In J. Greenberg and J. A. Colquitt (Eds.), *Handbook of organizational justice* (pp. 3–58). Erlbaum.

14. Cropanzano, R., Bowen, D. E., & Gilliland, S. W. (2007). The management of organizational justice. *Academy of Management Perspectives, 21*(4), 34–48.

15. Goodstein, J., & Butterfield, K. D. (2010). Extending the horizon of business ethics: Restorative justice and the aftermath of unethical behavior. *Business Ethics Quarterly, 20*(3), 453–480.

16. Espenson, J. (Story & Teleplay), St. John, T. (Story), & Whitmore, J. (Director). (1998). Gingerbread (Season 3, Episode 11) [TV series episode]. In *Buffy the Vampire Slayer.* Mutant Enemy Productions; 20th Century Fox Television.

17. Tripp, T. M., Bies, R. J., & Aquino, K. (2007). A vigilante model of justice: Revenge, reconciliation, forgiveness, and avoidance. *Social Justice Research, 20,* 10–34.

18. Chen, F. X., Graso, M., Aquino, K., Lin, L., Cheng, J. T., DeCelles, K., & Vadera, A. K. (2022). The vigilante identity and organizations. *Organizational Behavior and Human Decision Processes, 170,* 104136.

19. Teubner, G. (1991). The two faces of Janus: Rethinking legal pluralism. *Cardozo Law Review, 13,* 1443.

20. Humphrey, R. H. (2013). *Effective leadership: Theory, cases, and applications.* Sage Publications.

21. Goddard, D. (Writer), & Solomon, D. (Director). (2002). Selfless (Season 7, Episode 5) [TV episode]. In *Buffy the Vampire Slayer.* Mutant Enemy Productions.

22. Greenwalt, D. (Writer), & Whitmore, J. (Director). (1998). The Wish (Season 3, Episode 9) [TV series episode]. In *Buffy the Vampire Slayer.* Mutant Enemy Productions; 20th Century Fox Television.

10

FOLLOWERS MATTER TOO – XANDER'S X FACTOR

Here we are well into the 10th chapter of the book, and I figure it's the best possible juncture to talk about and discuss followership. One of the main criticisms of a lot of leadership books and scholarship out there is that there is scarcely if any discussion about followership. After all, good leaders need good followers in order to be effective. Think about a flawless surgeon who's performing a surgery (bariatric surgery for instance). That individual will need competent and effective followers for the surgery to be successful. Take a second and consider how effective Buffy would be were it not for the effective Scoobies like Willow and Xander (and later on Anya, Tara, and Dawn). Probably not very effective at all, right? In fact, there's a high likelihood that Buffy herself would not have survived past the first season.

So, it is imperative that one studies about followership as well when one is aiming to understand leadership. In fact, some would argue that it is more important to study followers than leaders, but I am not willing to go to that extreme. Instead, I will simply state that both are equally important, and a perfect tango between the two groups is what makes everyone tick together.[1-5] It's unfair to categorize one as being more important than the other; it's just that people have been more fascinated by leaders than followers because of the perception that it's easier to follow than it is to lead. That perception is rather faulty when you think of it, and in this chapter, I will discuss why followership is not exactly an easy process either. It can be quite difficult, truly.

In this chapter, I will start off by discussing what entails good followership, and how exactly the tango between leaders and followers can be a concordant one, and not one that feels like all individuals involved have multiple left legs. I will differentiate between the various kinds of followers out there, and I will illustrate and explain what category of followers' various characters from BtVS would be considered in. Next, I will discuss the X-factor of Xander because I really do think he was the ultimate follower in the Scooby Gang. Finally, I will discuss why followership is not exactly easier to do than leadership, as popularly believed. I will aim to use several different examples of characters from BtVS, regardless of the Xander-heavy symbology in the chapter title.

WHAT IS FOLLOWERSHIP... GOOD FOLLOWERSHIP?

Let's get one thing right out in the open and that is a brief discussion of the word followership. The word "follower" seems a bit impolite, but it really isn't. It's not demeaning to be a follower,[6,7] and nor is it a "banned word." It's not pejorative in the slightest – after all, you wouldn't want an entire platoon of leaders all leading together at the same time, would you? It'd be akin to an entire batch of monks from the Order of Dagon brewing up a dish together at the same time, each with his own recipe configuration. The eventual creation may not be anything remotely resembling the original recipe. So, it follows that it isn't a bad thing to be a follower – indeed, it's actually pretty important to be a follower at times. Follower basically refers to a person who adheres to the path that the leader has established. Research and factual evidence support the view that followers typically do a lot of the work that needs to be done. This percentage can vary from more than 50% to over 90% of the work.[8] That is the majority of the work itself. So, it's very important to have good followers since you do want your overall work to be good quality. If you have bad followers, the final product will probably be shoddy.

But back to the initial point about followers and followership. Basically, leaders would be unable to accomplish much if it were not for their followers, who have to do a major portion of the work. Most times, the leader is in charge of overall strategy, but the implementation of that strategy and the work involved falls on the shoulders of the followers. Should their shoulders be unequal to the task, then the overall strategy will fail, no matter how amazing the leader is. Think about the initiative in BtVS, where things started to fall apart for them, after the best follower of all in the initiative, Riley Finn, defected from the initiative.

While the death of Maggie Walsh could also be said to be instrumental in the eventual disbanding of the initiative, Riley's leaving was the first domino to fall, in a sense, and it was inevitable that the initiative would fail. One could argue that Riley was a leader of the initiative, and he probably was, but he was more a follower than a leader. He was a leader to several other followers, but he wasn't a leader of Maggie Walsh or anyone higher up. He was an excellent follower though and, indeed, showed a great aptitude for leadership, which he demonstrates amply in his time as an unofficial Scooby Gang member, and later on, as a demon-hunter for the US government. His brilliance as a follower was manifested in his ability to lead when necessary. Indeed, all good followers have this ability to switch roles when necessary and to stay in their lanes when required. Riley exemplified that attribute – when needed, he was happy to lead, and when needed, he was happy to follow.

That is the hallmark of good followers – the ability to switch roles and assume leader like positions when required. You can see that even in the Scooby Gang, where depending on the villain they're fighting, sometimes Buffy relinquishes control and power a bit, and someone else pitches in as a leader. Think about the time when all of the potential Slayers and even the Scoobies themselves were willing to let Faith lead the group against Caleb.[9] Almost a coup, it was, and while it did seem a bit ungrateful of them to have done that, it actually ended up being beneficial as it got the entire group together further committed to stopping Caleb and the First Evil. It also serves to bring forth the point that good followers (especially if they're working with good leaders) are not afraid to let their opinions be known to the leader. Let's now move on to the various subtypes of followers and discuss which subtypes several BtVS characters fit into.

TYPES OF FOLLOWERS

There are many ways to categorize followers, but I will be focusing on the Kellerman's five types of follower categorization.[10] It's an easy to understand and apply framework, so it makes the most sense to use that.

This model basically places followers into a continuum of follower types based on their respective levels of engagement. The first type, which is based on a complete or almost complete level of disengagement, is termed as an isolate follower.[9,10] These isolate followers hang about and do the bare minimum; in fact, sometimes not even the bare minimum but they skate by with impunity because they really don't care. The only recourse leaders can have here while dealing with isolates, especially if they are unable to coach them into being more engaged is to fire them. It may sound harsh to do that, but it may be the only thing that can prevent the isolate's disengagement from spreading.

Think about the followers who just don't get with the plan, and in fact, while they don't actively harm the leader's agenda, they don't help it either. If you look at this from an equity theory point of view,[11,12] these isolate followers would be classified as experiencing over-equity. They're getting the same resources and benefits that others are, for a fraction of the effort or enthusiasm. From BtVS though, it's a bit hard to pick any one person or group as being isolate followers. I would probably pick the futile soldiers (i.e., the ones who weren't really named) in the initiative as being isolate followers. While they were all supposedly involved in the initiative's mission, none of them were particularly enthusiastic or skilled about the mission. I suppose, an uncharitable way of describing them would be as cannon or fang and claw fodder. For the case of isolate followers, as hard as it is for me to admit, I do think that a Principal Snyder approach actually works out well. If you recall, in the BtVS series, Principal Snyder is perhaps the most Theory X kind of leader, and treats most students with disdain and sarcasm, as though he's convinced that they're wasting time and not engaged. Recall his dialog about discipline being exactly what kids need? That quality, that is, discipline, is precisely what leaders need to use to handle isolate followers. You either change them into a more useful follower or you get them to leave, or as Principal Snyder would do, expel them from the school or group or company.

Moving on from isolate followers (and let's face it, isolates will probably be happy to see people move on from them; they're really that checked out), let's get to the next follower type namely bystanders.[9] This group isn't as bad as the isolates, but they'd still probably get the Principal Snyder treatment, or at least, a tapered down version of Principal Snyder. This type of follower usually doesn't put in a whole lot of effort into doing much either, but unlike the isolates, they at least show up for meetings, etc., if only to gulp down pots of tea, and nibble ravenously on the free sandwiches. If they are interested in the overall mission, then they're a lot more likely to do things for their group. Spike in the early days of his embedded chip circuitry situation could be considered a bystander. He was typically uninvolved and uninterested unless he saw there was something in it for him. Again, this type of follower isn't as bad as the isolates, but leaders and groups don't exactly benefit from bystanders. Similar to the bystander effect, where when a crisis happens, some people just hang about doing nothing confident in the knowledge that someone else will take care of it. In situations like that, bystanders are as useless as an attempt to canoe away in the middle of a desert.

Next, we come to the more moderately active follower types suitably called participants.[9,13] These are the kinds of followers that make active engagement and choices to make a difference. They may, however, act contrary to what the leader wants, in that, they could take a stand that goes against what the leader wants. A great example or rather examples here would be all of the potential Slayers. In the very beginning, right after they're rescued by the Scooby Gang from being killed by Caleb or any of the First Evil's other confederates, they're almost like bystanders of a sort. But then they grow into becoming true participants (most of them), where they start to train and improve their fighting skills, not just to survive but to hopefully win in the battle against the First Evil (including battling with the Turok-Han or the Ubervamps). These followers are an excellent sort for leaders to canvas out because they are engaged, and the leader doesn't have to waste too much time in motivating them. That way the focus can be more on coaching them to be better performers similar to what we saw with the potential Slayers.

The next type of followers on that continuum are termed as activists.[9] This lot are a whole lot more committed and dedicated to the cause than are participants. They display a high degree of enthusiasm for the mission, and in some cases, that can lead them to disagree with their leader. Activist followers can be excellent followers, but they can also become pains in the jugular, by basically engaging in activism. Think about Kennedy from the potential Slayers – while the rest of the potential Slayers stayed put as participants, Kennedy really shone through and became an activist. One unpleasant encounter she was involved in revolved around training Chloe, where Kennedy was unduly harsh in the training to Chloe, and called her a maggot. This harsh treatment coupled with the First Evil's insidious whispering into Chloe's ear led Chloe to commit suicide. While one cannot entirely blame Kennedy for the suicide, she still bears some responsibility for that. If she hadn't been so harsh, perhaps, Chloe would have resisted the First Evil's psychological whisper campaign. So, in a sense, Kennedy was an activist follower bordering on the extreme. Again, this type of follower can be troublesome if they start to disagree with the leader, but, on the other hand, they can also help refine a leader's strategy. It does require fine-tuning though, quite a bit of it.

The final category of follower on the continuum of engagement is termed as diehards. These are extreme followers who are willing to go the distance and are willing to sacrifice themselves or their leader for the cause they believe in. Several characters in BtVS could be said to fit the bill here. Consider Caleb for instance – he could be said to be possibly one of the most diehard followers of the First Evil's. He was willing to do anything going as far as murdering entire groups of people (e.g., the entire Watcher's Council, and many potential Slayers). But one thing to be careful about is that when leaders have diehards as followers, there is a good chance that those diehards could end up usurping the leader's position because they're all of a sudden not impressed by the leader's strategies anymore. This doesn't happen with Caleb, but had he gotten to becoming more powerful, it is a possibility.

So, these five types of followers are typically what a leader might expect to see in an organization. Depending on the circumstances, there may be unique times when it would be better to have diehards or activists as compared to regular old participants. But I fail to imagine any situation where leaders would want bystanders or isolates as followers. That would be quite a draining experience, really. But honestly, I feel that the ideal sort of follower any leader would love to have would be the ones who'd be classified as participants. A sweet sort of spot to be in, not too little not too much, but just right. Let's now discuss the X-factor of Xander.

THE X-FACTOR OF XANDER

Xander was always one of the best things about the show – he brought with him a sense of joy, and his flippant sarcastic and self-deprecating take on matters, even serious, always had an uplifting sort of effect on the Scoobies.

Well okay, maybe not too much for Giles or Tara, but significantly so for Buffy, Willow, and Dawn. And Anya, of course, was majorly in love with him, till she got furious with him, but even then, she retained a soft spot for him. The reason I wanted to specifically discuss Xander in the context of this chapter is that among all the people in the Scooby Gang, I would personally consider Xander to be the best follower of all. He had no magical powers or superhuman strength, but he had an indomitable sense of loyalty, which is an amazing trait for any follower to have.

His indomitable loyalty was instrumental in getting the Scooby Gang through some really difficult times. As I've mentioned before, he was instrumental in getting Willow to back down from her rampage as Dark Willow. It took Xander's love and his loyalty to get her to snap back to reality and let go of the rage that had completely consumed her. This X-factor of Xander is something that any leader would die to have among his or her followers. And mind you, it's not the mindless sort of loyalty where they just jump when asked to (i.e., not like the mindless loyalty as displayed by Glory's minions, who would never question or challenge any of her decisions or wishes). Xander while loyal was also not immune to questioning either Buffy or Giles or Willow or anyone else, if he thought their plan was incorrect or their strategy was going to be a flop.

I believe that the type of follower leaders should be trying to get should be molded from the Xander Harris mold – loyal to a fault but not mindlessly so like a minion. Alright, one lone exception would be when Xander got hypnotized by Dracula to become a servant himself,[14] but that is an exception, and not Xander's actual state of being. Basically, loyalty coupled with courage – that is the X-factor that Xander possesses, and the ideal kind of follower any leader ought to be hoping to work with or lead. Now let's get to the question of whether it's easy to be a follower as compared to being a leader.

IS IT TRULY EASIER TO FOLLOW THAN LEAD?

Back to the original question – is it truly easy to follow rather than lead? An old story I remember hearing from a dearly departed professor of mine (Dr. David Lemak) was that there were 100 applicants for a particular position, and 99 of them said that they wanted to be effective leaders, but just 1 individual said they wanted to be an effective follower. The 1 individual ended up getting that position. While the anecdote may be a bit apocryphal, the sentiment behind it has a certain logic to it. Most people want to become leaders primarily due to the prestige factor, but there's also the secondary factor that leading is considered to be more challenging and following is supposed to be easier.

That is absolutely incorrect – people can, of course, have preferences for either leading or following, but anyone thinking that following is an easy task, should disabuse themselves of that. If you happen to be an engaged sort of follower, so maybe a participant or an activist type of follower, and your leader happens to be a complete nitwit. It will be quite hard for you to even consider following any foolish or absurd orders or rules flung your way. Similarly, if your leader is someone like Glory or the Master, your job as a follower will be even more stressful, and it'll be like walking a tightrope over a cliff at all times.

So, it's definitely not an easy task to be a follower; depending on what kind of leader you end up with, your job as a follower could be mind boggling in terms of complexity or difficulty. The minions of Glory could never ever stand up to her because they were so terrified of her wrath, and similarly, the followers of Harmony were a bit fed up of her gross incompetence. Not very pleasant for either group of followers, come to think of it. So, while being a follower does lack the glamor of being a leader, it does not imply that it's an easy job. It's important, but it doesn't have to be easy – the only situation where it is possibly easy is if you're a bystander, but that does get old real fast. Being a bystander cannot be a permanent occupation. At some point, you have to either quit or upgrade your level of engagement to become a better follower.

SUMMARY

In this chapter, I discussed followership, in terms of how it is important, and how many different types of followers there are. Additionally, I then discuss Xander's X-factor, which I liken to courage with loyalty. After which I also discuss how it is not necessarily easier to follow than it is to lead – sometimes, it can be incredibly hard to be a follower, so it's not just an easy route to take to avoid difficulty. In the next chapter, I will be discussing loneliness and how it relates to leadership.

REFERENCES

1. Chung, F. L., & Chung, H. H. (2021). The importance of followership in human resources. *Performance Improvement Quarterly, 34*(3), 261–277.

2. Matshoba-Ramuedzisi, T., De Jongh, D., & Fourie, W. (2022). Followership: A review of current and emerging research. *Leadership & Organization Development Journal, 43*(4), 653–668.

3. Jiang, X., Snyder, K., Li, J., & Manz, C. C. (2021). How followers create leaders: The impact of effective followership on leader emergence in self-managing teams. *Group Dynamics: Theory, Research, and Practice, 25*(4), 303.

4. Shen, L., & Abe, T. (2023). How do followership behaviors encourage job performance? A longitudinal study. *Current Psychology, 42*(17), 14652–14662.

5. Matthews, S. H., Kelemen, T. K., & Bolino, M. C. (2021). How follower traits and cultural values influence the effects of leadership. *The Leadership Quarterly, 32*(1), 101497.

6. Bunch, W. (2012). On being "just" a follower: Rejecting the pejorative and pursuing a higher calling. *Journal of Applied Christian Leadership, 6*(1), 65–71.

7. Hoption, C., Christie, A., & Barling, J. (2012). Submitting to the follower label: Followership, positive affect, and extra-role behaviors. *Zeitschrift für Psychologie, 220*(4), 221–230.

8. Dubrin, A. J. (2022). *Leadership research findings, practice and skills.* Dreamtech Press.

9. Kellerman, B. (2007). What every leader needs to know about followers. *Harvard Business Review, 85*(12), 84–145.

10. Danielsson, E. (2013). The roles of followers: An exploratory study of follower roles in a Swedish context. *Leadership & Organization Development Journal, 34*(8), 708–723.

11. Pritchard, R. D. (1969). Equity theory: A review and critique. *Organizational Behavior and Human Performance, 4*(2), 176–211.

12. Huseman, R. C., Hatfield, J. D., & Miles, E. W. (1987). A new perspective on equity theory: The equity sensitivity construct. *Academy of Management Review, 12*(2), 222–234.

13. Benson, A. J., Hardy, J., & Eys, M. (2016). Contextualizing leaders' interpretations of proactive followership. *Journal of Organizational Behavior, 37*(7), 949–966.

14. Noxon, M. (Writer), & Solomon, D. (Director). (2000). Buffy vs. Dracula (Season 5, Episode 1) [TV series episode]. In *Buffy the Vampire Slayer.* Mutant Enemy Productions; 20th Century Fox Television.

11

WILLOW WALK ALONE?
LEADERS AND LONELINESS

The 11th chapter is here, and in this one, we're going to be discussing loneliness in the context of leadership. I've always felt that leaders have to grapple with a special kind of loneliness. You could be surrounded by swathes of people and yet feel alone. I know many CEOs and CFOs and Corporate Directors, and this is one common theme they've all told me over the years. Their journeys can be so awfully lonely, and there's really not many people who can connect with or speak with them on specific to leadership issues, other than other leaders. That got me thinking about so many leadership books that lack any discussion of loneliness whatsoever, and I've always felt that to be a pity.

So, to make up for that lacunae, I really did want to write a chapter on leaders and loneliness. From a BtVS perspective, it really resonates with so many of the situations that Buffy, Faith, Willow, etc., have had to face throughout the series. Loneliness is not something that has no recourse though; there are solutions and protective measures leaders can take to stave off their loneliness. But it is important to acknowledge that loneliness is an issue that does inescapably appear in a leadership, and leaders need to be prepared to face it and handle it when it does loom up during their journeys.

In this chapter, I will first discuss what exactly loneliness is and what sort of implications it has for leadership. Following that I will discuss how loneliness affected many of our beloved BtVS Scooby Gang members, and if so how exactly their loneliness affected them. Then I will discuss why it is important for leaders to acknowledge that they will inevitably feel loneliness at one point or another; the ostrich strategy of failing to recognize a symptom or danger has never worked, and it doesn't work for loneliness either. So, let's start off with what exactly loneliness is in a leadership context.

L&L IS FOR LONELINESS & LEADERSHIP

Astute Hawaiian cuisine aficionados will recognize the homage in the section title, but for the purposes of the chapter, I'm referring to loneliness and leadership. Loneliness has been deemed as a societal epidemic and a nasty problem that affects people from across the globe.[1-2] You have entire societies grappling with increasing number of people feeling isolated and alone despite being surrounded by people. Historically, Weber[3] had predicted that increasing levels of bureaucratization would end up creating individuals who were practically "dehumanized." To me that overall dehumanization is ramped up manifold when it comes to leaders. After all, leaders are usually perceived as being separate from their flock, different and better than the folks they lead, etc. The very function of the role they occupy puts distance between them and followers (hark back to the power chapter), aptly termed as power distance.

The definition of loneliness that I think is a good one to use is to think of it as a distressing reaction to a perceived deficiency in social or personal relationships.[4-7] That explains why some people are not lonely even if they're alone because they're happy with their existing social or personal relationships, while others are decidedly unhappy even if they're surrounded by others. For leaders, this is especially acute because of role boundaries. Let's imagine that you are a jolly good old vampire strutting about in joy, and you are friends with another younger vampire. Suddenly, your friend gets handpicked by the Master to be the head of a certain vampire faction, thus rendering a really wide gap in your two statuses. Both of you will be likely to feel loneliness because the new role differentiation that exists will make it hard for you to be able as free with each other as you were.

That role gap in leader–follower relationships is the primary cause for leader loneliness. After all, the leader is no longer one of the boys or one of the girls but is instead now at a higher perch. Additionally, it can be quite difficult to be someone's boss or leader and yet be all buddy–buddy with them. A natural awkward distance unfortunately creeps in. Once loneliness creeps in, there are adaptive ways[8] to respond to it, which basically entail the lonely individual taking steps to socially connect with others. Sadly, due to the power distance and resultant social stratification and role gap, the people with whom you could fraternize with pre-leader status are now off limits. So, the typical adaptive solution is no longer available and doesn't work anymore. Think about if Spike permanently got the gem of Amara[9] embedded in him and could, therefore, walk about in blazing sunshine all the time; he would have probably gotten even more alienated from other vampires and gotten lonelier (although I must admit Spike was able to deal with loneliness a lot better than many other characters).

One of the biggest implications of loneliness for leaders is that now that they have no real choices to stave off their loneliness from among their followers. So, they do need to look for other ways by which to reduce or eliminate loneliness, or at least to make peace with that distressing emotion. Now, I will dive into a bit more detail in terms of how our BtVS characters dealt with loneliness, and whether or not they did a reasonable job doing so.

THE SCOOBY GANG'S EXPERIENCES OF LONELINESS

While the chapter title suggests it will be Willow Rosenberg heavy, I felt that it would be a pity to only focus on her, since after all, one would not want her to be *lonely* in this chapter either. Let's start off with Buffy first – as the titular Slayer of our series, Buffy acutely felt a lot of loneliness throughout the series. Several times in the series, she had to pretty much be willing to sacrifice herself to prevent an apocalypse or save one of her friends or family members. Right off the bat, the fact that she was the Slayer made her feel acutely lonely because she felt isolated in the battle against evil. People could help her or support her, but they would never truly feel the responsibility that she felt every living moment.

Similarly, due to her role as Slayer, Buffy never quite got to experience a normal life. Where others had to just face normal issues like who to invite to prom, or how to get into a club or group, Buffy had to not only sacrifice that but also had to be constantly focused on how to prevent vampires and demons from killing innocent ordinary people. The Scooby Gang and her Watcher Giles were immensely useful doubtless, but they couldn't quite experience what Buffy experienced. So, all she really got was a semblance of normalcy not the real deal though. Recall the time when Buffy first tells her mother Joyce that she's the vampire Slayer, and Joyce's response is utter befuddlement and a plaintive response that Buffy try and stop being a vampire Slayer. Buffy then directly speaks about how she's never had a normal life and feels so lonely, and finally, Joyce lashes out at her at the end of it while trying to stop her and warning her to not leave or forget about coming back.[10]

That scene was a bit of a shocker because while it was said in a moment of high emotion, and immediately regretted, it did bring to light the loneliness that Buffy chronically felt. Also, the fake murder allegation that was dangling over her head, with Snyder threatening to expel her, couldn't have been very pleasant, considering she couldn't even fight the allegations without revealing her Slayer status to the authorities. Buffy's loneliness was even further impacted by the many losses she faced – the loss of Angel when he became Angelus and had to be stabbed during the Acathla battle, poignantly changing to Angel just a second before getting stabbed by the blessed sword. Coming on the heels of her heated interaction with Joyce, that led to Buffy leaving town. In a sense, Angel's death was the last straw on her cake of loneliness pushing her into skipping town and her family and friends.

Now let's switch gears to Willow, the titular character of this chapter. Unlike Buffy, she's not really a leader in the initial couple of seasons and really starts getting into the leader role after discovering her penchant for magic and after getting more comfortable with her self-identity. But you can see the loneliness inherent in Willow throughout her tenure on the show. From the beginning, her loneliness is also deeply tied in with her romantic relationship failures. First, it's her unrequited love with Xander, next it's her broken relationship with Oz, and finally, Tara. While it's mostly great with Tara that also hits a roadblock at first due to Tara's concern about Willow's addiction to magic, and then later on, due to Warren's botched assassination of Buffy.

The loneliness still persists for Willow even after she returns from her magical rehabilitation in England. Due to circumstances involving Gnarl, neither Willow nor her friends could see one another. I thought that really accentuated and showed that Willow was super lonely despite having loved people around. Her loneliness was really severely impacted by her constant guilt and regret for the damage she did during her time as Dark Willow.

And the absence of Tara is a steady reminder to Willow that she must walk her path alone. It only starts to reduce a bit after the Summers' house becomes a camp like atmosphere filled with all of the potential Slayers.

Another character who you can tell really struggles with her loneliness is Dawn, Buffy's younger sister. You can tell that she too appears to have issues with loneliness right from the start. It gets worse once everyone knows that she was the key that Glory was seeking, and the Order of Dagon basically inserted Dawn into everyone's memories and timelines. Dawn herself is always plagued with this feeling of not belonging to the group, and when Joyce passes, and Buffy is all distracted by events, Dawn starts to make poor choices such as shoplifting from various stores (including The Magic Box, which Anya is super upset about) and lying to everyone around as well. She's finally caught in the episode titled *Older and Far Away*.[11]

Dawn basically feels left out of everything that the other Scoobies are involved in, and this doesn't do wonders for her constant feeling of loneliness. In fact, when you think of it, only Spike (and Xander) really treats her with a lot more closeness than several others in the Scooby Gang. Spike, in particular, always welcomes Dawn to his crypt for a chat, which speaks volumes about Dawn's comfort level with him. A disappointing situation that happens is when Dawn is convinced that she is a potential Slayer, but then it turns out that Willow's spell which passed through Dawn was seeking out Amanda (who was the real potential Slayer). You will remember reading about this previously when I wrote about how Xander comforts her and expresses his own feelings about being the non-powered member of the group. Xander's "super-power" of being a person who notices things actually makes Dawn feel so much better, and dare I say it, a bit less lonely.[12]

Now just for varieties sake, I am going to write about a non-human character (namely Spike) and his loneliness. When we see him in the beginning after he first arrives on the scene along with Drusilla,[13] he's the epitome of bad boy'ness (not sure if that's a real word, but the English language is always expanding, so we might as well get in on the ground floor of this one). Spike seems fairly equanimous with his lonely existence, and I guess most vampires could be said to follow that mold pattern. Angel too even though supremely broody could be said to not let the loneliness really affect him too adversely.

We start to see Spike's craving for community around the time he starts to hang out more with the Scooby Gang and starts to fall in obsessive love with Buffy. In one of the icky parts of the BtVS series, we can see one of the consequences of Spike's unhealthy obsession with Buffy, as he gets Warren to create a Buffybot,[14] which was basically a robotic replica of Buffy (do note that the presence of the Buffybot created a lot of comedic yet icky misunderstandings for others, as they'd mistake the robot for the real Buffy). Spike's loneliness manifested itself with his increasing obsession with Buffy, which eventually came to a zenith when he decided he wanted to be ensouled again to be able to win over Buffy.

There are more BtVS characters I could write about here that also experienced and felt acute loneliness, but I think it is time to get to the next section, namely, the importance of leaders acknowledging loneliness, and to avoid the ostrich response of ignoring problems till they definitely never go away.

ACKNOWLEDGE LONELINESS...

At the very outset here, let me clarify that the ostrich effect I alluded to earlier on does a bit of disservice to actual real-life ostriches. The birds in discussion do not really bury their heads in the sand to avoid danger – that is a misattribution to the poor giant bird by over-imaginative Roman historians. But regardless, the metaphor has become so pervasive that the ostrich effect is easily understood to be a situation where someone ignores negative news or information about dangerous problems, etc. Basically, such individuals simply do not acknowledge their problems and think that if they ignore the problems, they'll go away. So, apologies to the ostrich community, but unfortunately the metaphor has become so widely known that there is simply no way to rename it after any other suitable animal species. But back to our topic of acknowledging loneliness. As I've discussed already, loneliness is a pervasive feeling of distress and leaders definitely feel it, simply by virtue of their role.

As the various examples in the previous section emphasize, different individuals have different responses to loneliness, and some seem to be better equipped to handle it, while others struggle to respond to it. The ones who struggle to respond to loneliness or fail to respond at all fall prey to the cardinal sin of failing to acknowledge loneliness. It can be hard to admit that you're feeling lonely, especially if you're a leader and only have interactions with followers or people who simply are unable to process the same emotions or experience the same kind of experiences. So, the first step is to acknowledge that you are experiencing loneliness, and next, to do something about it.

A good example to use here about a BtVS character that truly accepts his own sense of loneliness is good old Rupert Giles. If anyone should be lonely in the series, it ought to be Giles. He spends his time mentoring and hanging out with kids, and apart from a short tryst with Joyce and a bit longer but still short romantic entanglement with Jenny Calendar (who was brutally killed by Angelus), Giles has been shown throughout the series as being rather lonely. However, he does not mope around and fret due to the loneliness – compared to any of the other characters, Giles show a great deal of emotional self-sufficiency. He to me appears to be the one who best accepts his chronic sense of loneliness.

While I am not advocating that leaders, who experience loneliness embrace the entire persona of Giles (at least not completely, wearing a Gilesian wardrobe wouldn't be too bad), I am suggesting that they borrow some of his attitude regarding loneliness. Unlike the other BtVS characters, Giles is not too badly fussed about his loneliness. He accepts that a certain amount of loneliness comes built in due to the responsibilities of his position of Watcher and mentor to the vampire Slayer. "He accepts" is the key phrase here – leaders need to be able to accept the loneliness they will feel in their roles as leaders, just like Giles did. I would add here that perhaps introverts are better able to handle this loneliness than are extroverts; but again, that's not going to be true of every single introvert or extrovert out there.

The leaders I know and have conversed with about this topic have told me that while they have accepted loneliness they have not accepted ignoring it (or pretending that it doesn't exist). Instead what a lot of these leaders do is to seek out executive coaches or peer mentors (these tend to be other leaders, either retired or active in the field) with whom they discuss their loneliness. These executive coaches or peer mentors don't have to be from the same industry or company, but they do have to be leaders. At the risk of sounding like an elitist Watcher, I will have to say here that executive coaches ought to have leadership experience themselves. You cannot talk someone through their loneliness spells if you haven't actually experienced it or faced it or handled it yourself.

Imagine how silly it would be for Giles to go confiding in Manna Rocha (from the Doublemeat Palace) or Principal Snyder and seeking recourse from them. Neither Manny nor Snyder would understand and nor they would have any useful advice for Giles. A better choice would be to reach out to someone else more equipped for that discussion, someone like another fellow Watcher perhaps, or even someone practiced in magic. Why, even D'Hoffryn might make for a decent coach or mentor, although there is a danger of getting co-opted into becoming a vengeance demon in the process.

But it all starts with acceptance and acknowledgement of loneliness. Leaders have to acknowledge that the position they're in entails a fantastic amount of responsibility, which precludes them from truly being able to open up with their followers. That's where the loneliness starts, and then any leader actions or behaviors that could be unpopular further worsen the loneliness. So, unless leaders come in to their roles fully aware that they are going to experience crushing amounts of loneliness, and they have to accept that. If not, then they may be unable to handle it. After acknowledging the loneliness, leaders have a choice – they can either embrace the Gilesian method of not caring too much for it, and being emotionally self-sufficient, or to seek out mentors or leadership coaches that can help them handle or face the loneliness.

Speaking of Buffy, one aspect that really helped her handle or acknowledge her loneliness was the responsibility and duty aspect of her position (similar to Giles). She knew that without her services and responsibilities as Slayer, the town would be overrun with demons and vampires. So, she made her peace with the loneliness side of things (not as flawlessly as Giles, but she did eventually). Come to think of it, so too did Faith, who perhaps was even lonelier than Buffy. She was also accepting of her loneliness, and that's really all a lonely leader can do – acknowledge it, and either accept it or deal with it by talking about it with coaches or peer-mentors.

SUMMARY

In this chapter, I discussed loneliness, and how it affects leaders in particular due to their role as leader, and the responsibilities such roles demand. I also discuss several examples of BtVS characters to explain how loneliness affected them in their own journeys. Finally, I discuss how leaders must acknowledge loneliness inherent in their leadership journeys and use Giles mostly to explain that. In the next chapter, we're going to be hurtling toward the end, as the 12th chapter will be the final one. Not quite hellmouth opening or mayoral ascension or Acathla raising type material, but still, it ought to be a good one. So, let's move along to Chapter 12 now.

REFERENCES

1. Killeen, C. (1998). Loneliness: An epidemic in modern society. *Journal of Advanced Nursing*, *28*(4), 762–770.

2. Jeste, D. V., Lee, E. E., & Cacioppo, S. (2020). Battling the modern behavioral epidemic of loneliness: Suggestions for research and interventions. *JAMA Psychiatry*, *77*(6), 553–554.

3. Stivers, R. (2004). *Shades of loneliness: Pathologies of a technological society*. Rowman & Littlefield Publishers.

4. Lam, H., Giessner, S. R., Shemla, M., & Werner, M. D. (2024). Leader and leadership loneliness: A review-based critique and path to future research. *The Leadership Quarterly*, *35*, 101780.

5. Silard, A., & Wright, S. (2020). The price of wearing (or not wearing) the crown: The effects of loneliness on leaders and followers. *Leadership*, *16*(4), 389–410.

6. Gabriel, A. S., Lanaj, K., & Jennings, R. E. (2021). Is one the loneliest number? A within-person examination of the adaptive and maladaptive consequences of leader loneliness at work. *Journal of Applied Psychology*, *106*(10), 1517.

7. Chen, X., Peng, J., Lei, X., & Zou, Y. (2021). Leave or stay with a lonely leader? An investigation into whether, why, and when leader workplace loneliness increases team turnover intentions. *Asian Business & Management*, *20*, 280–303.

8. McCarthy, J. M., Erdogan, B., Bauer, T. N., Kudret, S., & Campion, E. (2025). All the lonely people: An integrated review and research agenda on work and loneliness. *Journal of Management*, 01492063241313320.

9. Espenson, J. (Writer), & Contner, J. A. (Director). (1999). The Harsh Light of Day (Season 4, Episode 2) [TV series episode]. In *Buffy the Vampire Slayer*. Mutant Enemy Productions; 20th Century Fox Television.

10. Whedon, J. (Writer & Director). (1998). Becoming, Part 2 (Season 2, Episode 22) [TV episode]. In *Buffy the Vampire Slayer*. Mutant Enemy Productions.

11. Greenberg, D. Z. (Writer), & Gershman, M. (Director). (2002). Older and Far Away (Season 6, Episode 14) [TV series episode]. In *Buffy the Vampire Slayer*. Mutant Enemy Productions; 20th Century Fox Television.

12. Kirshner, R. R. (Writer), & Contner, J. A. (Director). (2003). Potential (Season 7, Episode 12) [TV series episode]. In *Buffy the Vampire Slayer*. Mutant Enemy Productions; 20th Century Fox Television.

13. Greenwalt, D. (Story & Teleplay), & Whedon, J. (Story). (1997). School Hard (Season 2, Episode 3) [TV series episode]. In *Buffy the Vampire Slayer*. Mutant Enemy Productions; 20th Century Fox Television.

14. Espenson, J. (Writer), & Gershman, M. (Director). (2001). Intervention (Season 5, Episode 18) [TV series episode]. In *Buffy the Vampire Slayer*. Mutant Enemy Productions; 20th Century Fox Television.

12

CONCLUSION – HOW TO BE THE QUINTESSENTIAL SLAYER

All good things come to an end, and sadly BtVS the series did too. After seven glorious seasons, it ended, leaving behind legions of fans, who still had an appetite for all things Buffy or Scooby Gang related. Yours truly was one of those fans, so it's been quite marvelous getting to write a book that is based on the BtVS series. And by now, most of those fans including me are perhaps ecstatic to learn that a reboot of BtVS is on its way, with Sarah Michelle Gellar returning as Buffy (although maybe she'll be the new Giles in this version, couldn't say for sure). Still early days in terms of details about the reboot (although I do expect those of you reading this book in the future after it's out in print will know all the nitty gritty details already). But yes, all good things come to an end, and this book is about to as well.

In this chapter, I will essentially be cobbling together various elements discussed in other previous chapters of this book, and distilling it all into a concluding chapter, which will give individuals and aspiring leaders ideas on how they too can become quintessential Slayers and be able to vanquish the vampires, demons, and werewolves of ineffective leadership. Basically, everyone has the potential to become a Slayer, but not everyone will be able to without having the tools to doing so at their disposal. This chapter intends to discuss those tools in a specific cogent way. Anyone aspiring to be an effective leader would do well to learn and bring in these various tools to his or her Slayer kit.

Again, effective leadership is about leading in a way such that whatever mission or goals you have are accomplished. In Slayer parlance, what that means is that as an effective leader, you have got to be able to accomplish your goals such as protecting your people, and adhering to your responsibility and sense of duty. Effective Slayers don't abandon their posts and leave their people behind, and neither should effective leaders. In this final and 12th chapter, I will examine the themes inherent in all of the previous chapters and provide additional insights on how individuals can use this material to improve their own Slayer potential. So, let's get started now with discussing the major themes in the book, shall we?

SLAYERS MUST BE POWERFUL, PERSUASIVE, AND RESPONSIBLE

As you will recall, the second chapter was all about power and persuasion, while the third chapter delved (this word has not been written by Chat GPT, I assure you!) into responsibility. Throughout the various chapters of this book, the responsibility theme is one that is perhaps present either obliquely or directly throughout. In BtVS, we typically see that the characters we grow to love are firmly on the side of responsibility (i.e., be it Buffy or Giles or Xander, etc.). The antagonists typically don't show a whole lot of responsibility (consider Faith for instance, or even Willow when she was Dark Willow), and while some do grow into being more responsible, their initial irresponsibility sticks on with them, and the stain never quite goes away completely. Therefore, in order to be an effective leader, strive to do your best to be responsible for your role, for your organization, and most importantly, for the people you lead. That stain of irresponsibility can fade away, but isn't it better to not make a stain in the first place? Faith never really measured up to Buffy's stature as a leader, and that's because unlike Buffy, Faith was completely irresponsible and allied herself with some frankly evil people at different times.

Another attribute that is common in effective leaders is that of power. Effective leaders have to be powerful to be able to do the things that make them effective. If they lack power, then they will never be able to accomplish any of their goals. Let's take the example of Clem here – a good natured loose-skinned demon, but not a very powerful one. Clem might make for a perfect babysitter for Dawn, but if a situation involved use of power, he would not be the man or rather demon for the task. Effective leaders have to be powerful on the various bases of powers, if not all of them, at least some of them. For instance, consider Giles with his expertise power. He might not be able to fight and beat really seasoned vampires or demons (but he's no slouch with ordinary demons or vampires). He can accomplish that thanks to his prodigious knowledge of history and Watcher training (and his rather wild youth which had him living a rambunctious lifestyle, and going by the nickname Ripper).

Obtaining power should be a priority for leaders because power can aid them in persuading their followers into behaving or performing actions for them. Of course, if you're already a skilled master of persuasion, you could use that to increase or gain your power; but in my personal view, I think it's easier to get power and then persuade rather than persuade to get power. To use a BtVS example to illustrate that – imagine that you're hunting a vampire sans power. You will find that no matter how persuasive you are with your words, they alone will not succeed or be useful. However, if you have power, then it's a lot easier to persuade the vampire into doing something you want them to (like move into the sunlight for a wee bit).

Therefore, to sum up these three themes into a short paragraph is to state that potential effective Slayers (okay leaders) need to acquire and use power in order to be able to be persuasive leaders. Additionally, they must always use these powers and negotiation skills with a strong base on responsibility. Without responsibility in place, these leaders could end up taking drastic and counterintuitive steps, which could be supremely harmful. Both Dark Willow and Faith Lehane demonstrated that in ample quantities, since their actions were incredibly dangerous to others, primarily because of their actions being steeped in irresponsibility or at least an absence of responsibility if not outright irresponsibility.

IMMERSE THYSELF IN MENTORING AND ENSOULING (NOT TOO MUCH THOUGH)

I am not wholly sure why I used the above Ye Olde English in the section heading (hmm... no mind control hopefully by the trio of Warren, Jonathan, and Andrew), but it does lend a certain gravity to the matter. While I discussed mentorship in Chapter 4, many of the examples I've used in the book are about mentorship, again some in more oblique ways than others. I have always maintained that getting involved in the mentorship process can be life-changing and life-affirming. This does need to be genuine though – if it's perceived as being insincere, then the mentoring will be a total disaster. It'll be similar to the Hellions running town with nothing formidable to stop them. In other worse, while I do assert that aspiring Slayers engage in the mentoring process, I also assert that it is better to not engage in the mentoring process at all, if you're half-hearted about it. I've seen people sign up to be mentors and then never ever respond to the queries of those mentees, or do so uselessly or half-heartedly. What a tragic waste of everyone's time that is, isn't it? If you get to mentor someone do them the kindness and respect of being truly invested as a mentor in their growth. Think about how Buffy really threw her life on the line and mentored all of the potential Slayers. She killed the ubervamp or the Turok-Han right in front of the potential slayers to impress upon the potentials the gravity of the responsibility that Slayers are to have and to fight no matter how scared they may be.

And as mentors or mentees, leaders need to be able to walk the walk and not just talk it. Imagine if Giles hadn't accompanied Buffy on many of her rounds, or if he'd simply tossed her a book, and told her to study up on her own. That would have left her far from being prepared for her role, especially during the beginning when she was still inexperienced. I am certainly not suggesting that mentors need to be doing a lot of hand-holding throughout their times with their mentees – but I am suggesting that a bit of hand-holding may be necessary in the beginning. To be an effective mentor, be prepared to do a bit of hand-holding and more hands-on coaching, at least in the beginning.

Then for the ensouling aspect, essentially what that refers to is that leaders must be authentic and genuine. If a leader truly has no soul, then I suppose one will have to find the descendants of the Kalderash people and get them to perform an ensouling ritual or ritual of restoration, or do what Spike did and undergo a Demon Trials. Luckily though, most leaders around us probably (well maybe) aren't demons or vampires, so the ensoulment aspect pertinent to them only involves getting them to embrace their authenticity and become authentic leaders. As I've mentioned in detail in Chapter 5, authenticity helps one avoid suffering through emotional labor, and that itself is an enormous gain, and worth the price of admission.

The only thing to really worry about here is that leaders need to keep their authenticity from getting out of hand and making them zealots in the process. It's good to be authentic in your approach to life, but it's bad to be expecting others to have to zealously adhere to your authentic approach to life or work. Think about the "Return to Office" mandates that current business leaders are all seemingly crazy about. They're probably authentic in that they genuinely believe that employees work more productively in the office, but that authenticity of theirs is becoming zealot like because they're refusing to see the evidence of the benefits of flexible work-mode statuses, and ignoring the evidence that hybrid or remote employees are equally if not more productive than the at-office colleagues. In this case, to me, it appears that authenticity has gotten a bit out of hand. At least, be willing to change your opinions and strategies if evidence emerges that your position isn't optimal.

SLAYERS SHOULD ENCOURAGE SELF-LEADERSHIP AND KNOW THEIR IDENTITIES

In terms of self-leadership, leaders basically need to be able to guide their followers into individuals who are able to lead when required. They need to be empowered enough to be able to display self-leadership. In the Scooby Gang, even though Buffy was the Slayer, she wasn't averse to seeking out help from the rest of the Scoobies including Willow and Oz and Xander. Her allowing them to help, and empowering them, in a way, is what prepared them to become leaders in their own right on several occasions. So, leaders, don't throttle your team or followers, allow them to grow into being leaders themselves. Empower them, but do be a bit cautious about overburdening your team. Remember in the end, you're still the leader, so don't go about removing yourself from the situation completely. Be present and be visible, just don't be hovering over them like a famished vampire would over a bucket of fresh blood.

One of the most important strategies of self-leadership is the point about constructive thought pattern strategies. This is I believe supremely integral in becoming an effective Slayer or leader. You have to be optimistic and ready and willing to face adverse situations and times of utter dejection. Having the optimism to face them and be able to inspire others to think constructively is key here. In the entire battle against the First Evil, Buffy and the other Scoobies are constantly trying to model good behavior and constructive thought pattern strategies to the potentials, and even Faith does that in terms of constructive thought pattern strategies.

From the identity perspective, leaders must be aware and fully cognizant of their various layers of identity. They definitely must be able to switch between their identities to avoid a clash of identities since a clash of identities benefits nobody and nothing. Leaders should also be on the watch and guard against overidentification – identify with the identity that is most salient in a given situation. Buffy was the Slayer, but for a time, she was also a school counselor (thanks to Principal Wood, because she wasn't really qualified for the job), and when she was a school counselor, she had to use a different identity to counsel kids coming to speak with her. Yes, in some cases, she had to think or act with her Slayer hat, but in most other cases, she didn't have to think like a Slayer at all. Just like that, leaders should first be confident and aware of their own identities and be able to operate with the one that is most salient.

SLAYERS SHOULD STRIVE TO BE RESILIENT AND FORGIVING (ON OCCASION)

Resilience is a big factor in leader effectiveness, and Slayers and leaders should be equipped with copious amounts of resilience. You have got to be able to bounce back (or forward) from adverse outcomes or disappointing news, and not let that beat you down forever. If you face failure once or a few times, brush it off, learn from it, and go back and try again. Avoid letting temporary failure turn permanent – deny it the right to become a permanent fixture in your life. Be resilient like Buffy was throughout the series, or even how Xander and Faith were. They faced practically impossible odds, and the decks were stacked against them, but yet, they persisted and were rewarded for their resilience with eventual success. Resilience doesn't make guarantee success, but it at least gives you a good shot at averting permanent failure.

But on the flip side, leaders have to make sure that they are not falling into the trap of sunk cost fallacy. They should not be sticking on to a failed strategy because of an obsessive escalation of commitment. Sometimes, you just have to let go and write off your losses. That does not mean you're being non-resilient but resilience does not mean you keep trying the same losing battle over and over. Sometimes, you may have to abandon the plan and go do something else. We see Spike do this when the going gets too hot for comfort. Remember the time when he takes off to a "Southern American" country with Drusilla, knowing that he's lost that particular battle with Buffy. He was being clever in retreating then instead of sticking around and being resilient for no good reason.

In terms of forgiveness, leaders do need to be forgiving in order to let their employees and followers learn from mistakes. If a leader is way too unforgiving, then their followers will never improve and instead may start hiding facts to avoid being the messenger that gets shot. Buffy demonstrates great forgiveness herself when she doesn't just go about massacring demons and vampires indiscriminately. She is quite deliberate in choosing who to dust and who to leave unalive or undead (a bit difficult to pick a word here ever since unalive has entered the English language). And Anya, of course, despite being a vengeance demon is actually not too bad in the forgiveness department, lacking the hate and resolve to take revenge on Xander even though he broke her heart. Leaders should be big hearted enough to be able to forgive mistakes of their followers (at least the mistakes that are forgivable). Unforgivable mistakes coupled with a sheer lack of repentance obviously deserve a sharp stake to the heart, but for the others, there should be some grace thrown in.

SLAYERS NEED TO LOOK OUT FOR THEIR FOLLOWERS AND BE PREPARED FOR LONELINESS

Leaders ought to be cognizant that their success depends, to a large extent, on the premise that their followers are competent and motivated individuals. If a leader has poor quality and uninterested followers, that leader isn't going to be seeing much success. Imagine you are a vampire Slayer, and you have poor quality followers. Say, instead of Willow or Xander, you have incompetent Willow, who messes up simple research, and incompetent and uninterested Xander, who refuses to help out in any way. Then you're not going to be a very successful slayer, that's for sure.

Additionally, you have to try and cultivate followers who are not just blindly loyal but instead empowered enough to challenge you, if your plans are plain wrong or destined to fail, and you just happen to have your blinkers on, and are unable to truly see hidden-in-plain-sight dangers. You also need to realize that while being a leader is hard, being a follower can be equally hard if not harder. So, do give a bit of grace to your followers who question you and suggest tweaks to your plans – they're not just doing that to annoy you or to usurp your power. If they're showing their interest, then you should encourage that and be receptive to possible tweaks or plan changes/edits. Better to have participant followers than to have isolates or bystanders – no real gain to be gotten by having followers like that.

And then, we come to the big L of leadership, namely loneliness. This is something all leaders will experience inevitably in their journeys unless they're absolutely laissez-faire types who don't lift a finger to do any actual work. If anything, I would say that if a leader hasn't experienced at least some loneliness in their leadership journey, then their voyage hasn't really taken them very far, or they've never had to make an unpopular decision. Imagine being a witch and never having ever cast a spell – that's a similar situation in nature to a leader who's never experienced loneliness in his or her journey. The important thing here is for leaders to acknowledge the inevitable loneliness, and either accept it and make peace with it, or aim to resolve it by seeking out executive coaches who can help guide them through the lonely morass.

SUMMARY

This chapter sums up the book, by providing insights and lessons for Slayers… I mean leaders. These insights and lessons are not the only lessons leaders need to have of course, but they are a great start to being able to start to vanquish the forces of ineffective leadership. To avoid being an ineffective leader, you have to be able to be a responsible leader, who is acutely aware of his or her own identity, and forgiveness quotient, etc., among other attributes. And, being aware of one's followers is also a good goal to aim for because as is becoming increasingly well known; followers play a vital role in ensuring that leaders become successful and effective leaders.

As we finally embark on the conclusion of this book, I do sincerely hope that you, that is, the reader and other readers have learned something useful, and enjoyed reading the book. I'm assuming you are BtVS fans, so I do hope you enjoyed the BtVS context which is embedded throughout the book. I really do think that popular culture offers an incredible lens to discuss and learn about leadership. And the BtVS context continues to be an incredibly relevant context, aided by a vibrant community of BtVS fans and well-wishers. So, I really did enjoy writing this book, as it gave me the opportunity to go back and relive/rewatch the entire series again to refresh my memories and double down on the fact that I will continue to be a BtVS Scooby Gang member myself. And please do remember, when confronted with strange and alluring looking books, please *do not speak Latin* in front of them. I hope that you will strive to be an effective Slayer/leader yourselves, and I wish you all the best in your present and future endeavors. We've all got potential to be effective leaders, so let's not get swayed away by evil or incompetence lurking in all corners. Slay away with judiciousness!

APPENDIX: CHARACTERS FROM THE BUFFY THE VAMPIRE SLAYER SERIES REFERENCED IN THIS BOOK

Name	Brief Description
Adam	He was a cybernetic demonoid created by Professor Maggie Walsh of the initiative. He was the primary antagonist in season 4 and was played by George Hertzberg
Amy Madison	Amy was a witch, who the Scooby Gang saved from her mother's body switch. She actually spends a lot of time in the series as a rat, and when she does recover, is a bit of a rival and foil for Willow. She also tends to misuse her powers and is a bad influence for Willow. She was played by Elizabeth Anne Allen
Andrew Wells	Part of the Trio – the group of supervillain nerds or nerd supervillains. Andrew eventually has a redemption arc and ends up helping the Scooby Gang against the First Evil. He was played by Tom Lenk
Angelus/Angel	Angelus when he was a sadistic vampire, and Angel when he was a vampire with a soul (having been cursed by the Kalderash people to feel eternal remorse). He was Buffy's love interest in the first two seasons. He was also one of the primary antagonists in season 2. He was played by David Boreanaz
Anyanka/Anya Jenkins	She was a vengeance demon called Anyanka, and when she lost her powers, she became human albeit with demon manners when it came to directness and subtleties. She was Xander's love interest for several seasons and was almost married to him. She was played by Emma Caulfield
Buffy Summers	The series' titular vampire Slayer. Buffy is the main protagonist in the series and is one of the main reasons why Sunnydale hasn't been swept into the hellmouth or gotten stuck in a purgatory type of situation. She was played by Sarah Michelle Gellar
Caleb	Caleb was a defrocked priest and a serial killer who was a lieutenant of the First Evil. He was responsible for the bombing of the Watcher's Council and for orchestrating the deaths of several potential Slayers. He was played by Nathan Fillion

(*Continued*)

(*Continued*)

Name	Brief Description
Clem	He was an extremely friendly and harmless loose skinned demon. He was a friend of Spike and even got to become a friend of the Scoobies. He was played by James C. Leary
Cordelia Chase	She was initially portrayed as a "Bête Noire" of the Scoobies. A popular girl yet a mean one. Eventually, she becomes a girlfriend of Xander's and even helps the Scoobies on some occasions. Eventually though, she leaves to go join *Angel*, that is, the show. She was played by Charisma Carpenter
Darla	Darla is Angelus' sire and is a close affiliate of the Master. She gets a more sizeable role in the spinoff *Angel*. She was played by Julie Benz
Dawn Summers	She was the "Key" who got integrated into Buffy's and friends/family's lives as Buffy's younger sister. She is seen as the baby of the group but eventually becomes a really integral part of the group's research wing. She was played by the dearly departed Michelle Trachtenberg, who passed on February 26, 2025
D'Hoffryn	D'Hoffryn was the master of the vengeance demons, a group which included humans who were elevated to demonic status by D'Hoffryn, and given the powers to invoke revenge on behalf of people who felt like they deserved revenge. He was played by Andy Umberger
Drusilla	Drusilla was Spike's lover and also Spike's sire. She was a psychic in Victorian London, who was driven mad and turned into a vampire by Angelus. Drusilla sired Spike in her own turn. She was one of the primary antagonists in season 2. She was played by Juliet Landau
Faith Lehane	Faith is another vampire Slayer, who got activated after the death of Kendra (who in turn was activated after the temporary death of Buffy). Faith has had a damaged and turbulent childhood, which makes her a rather volatile character. She ends up allying with the evil Mayor Wilkins but eventually has a redemption arc of her own thanks to Angel (on his show). She was played by Eliza Dushku
First Evil	The First Evil was the main antagonist in season 7. It manifested from all existent evil but was non-corporeal and so was restricted to taking the form of any human who had died (even briefly, which is why it was able to impersonate Buffy). It was an expert in psychological manipulation
Glory/Glorificus	Glory or Glorificus was a god from a hell dimension and intent on finding the "key" in order to return back to her original home dimension. She was the main antagonist in season 5. She was played by Clare Kramer
Halfrek	Halfrek was a rival/friend of Anyanka's and was a fellow vengeance demon. Her main clientele consisted of neglected or abused children. She was played by Kali Rocha

(*Continued*)

Name	Brief Description
Harmony Kendall	While human she was a member of Cordelia's clique, even ending up taking over the clique once Cordy starts dating Xander. Eventually, she becomes a vampire and dates Spike (almost a one-sided relationship that eventually breaks). Harmony ends up being a regular on *Angel* later on. She was played by Mercedes McNab.
Jenny Calendar	She was the computer teacher at Sunnydale High School but was actually a member of the Kalderash Tribe who had sent her to Sunnydale to keep an eye on Angel. She is a techno-pagan, and becomes Giles' love interest, and is also one of Angelus' victims. She was played by Robia LaMorte
Jonathan Levinson	Another member of the infamous trio of supervillain nerds. Jonathan was the caster of spells in the trio, and while not as evil as Warren, still had several evil moments. He could have had a redemption arc, but that was cut short by the machinations of the First Evil. He was played by Danny Strong
Joyce Summers	Buffy and Dawn's mom. Joyce is a loving mother, but she does have her share of verbal jousts with Buffy, especially when it comes around schoolwork and Slayer duties. Joyce dies of natural causes in the series, and this leads Buffy to have to really adult up fast. She was played by Kristine Sutherland
Maggie Walsh	She was a Psychology Professor at the University of California, Sunnydale. But she was secretly the leader of the Initiative, a secret government sanctioned military project to capture, study, and modify the behavior of demons and other supernatural entities. She created Adam and was a mentor of Riley's. She was played by Lindsay Crouse
Oz aka Daniel Osbourne	Oz was Willow's first boyfriend and a member of the musical group *Dingoes Ate My Baby*. He was also a werewolf, and left Sunnydale, when he ended up cheating on Willow with a female werewolf (Veruca), and didn't trust himself to not hurt Willow again. He was played by Seth Green
Principal Robin Woods	Another Principal, noticeably less cranky and a lot more personable than Snyder. He was actually a son of a Slayer (Nikki Wood), who Spike had killed in 1977. He joined hands with Buffy and the rest in the fight against the First Evil. He was played by D.B. Woodside
Principal R. Snyder	One of the crankiest Principals of all time, and an authoritarian one. He eventually met his demise during the graduation battle with the Mayor. The R. continues to be a source of mystery; although in a non-canonical source, it was revealed that his name was Cecil. He was played by Armin Shimerman

(*Continued*)

(*Continued*)

Name	Brief Description
Quentin Travers	Quentin was a watcher, and the final director of the Watcher's Council. A strict and rigid man, he often clashed with Buffy and Giles. He ended up getting killed along with a majority of Watchers during Caleb's bombing of the Council headquarters. He was played by Harris Yulin
Richard Wilkins III aka Mayor Wilkins	The Mayor was the mayor of Sunnydale and also an evil being intent on becoming a demon in a process termed as an Ascension. He has an almost father-like relationship with Faith Lehane and is eventually killed when the library rigged with explosives is set off. He was the primary antagonist of season 3 of BtVS
Riley Finn	Riley was a soldier working for the Initiative and also posing as a teaching assistant for Professor Walsh at UW Sunnydale. He was also Buffy's only "normal" boyfriend for quite a while, till they breakup. Eventually, he goes on to be married to someone else and continues to work for the government as a demon hunter. He was played by Mark Blucas
Rupert Giles	Giles was the librarian at Sunnydale High School and also the Watcher of Buffy. He was also a mentor and surrogate father figure of Buffy's (and some of the other Scoobies too, one must say). He had a wild side during his days of youth when he went by Ripper. He was played by Anthony Stewart Head
The Master	The Master was the main antagonist of season 1. He was an ancient vampire who was devoted to the cause of eradicating humanity and believed that he would fulfill a prophecy that he would kill the Slayer. He was played by Mark Metcalf
Spike aka William Pratt	Spike was a vampire sired by Drusilla, who took pity of a sort on William Pratt, a sobbing broken-hearted poet in the Victorian era. He was infamous for having killed two past Slayers. He started off as one of the main antagonists in season 2, but then had a redemption arc, and ended up as Buffy's romantic interest. He was played with delectable style by James Marsters
Tara Maclay	Tara is another member of the Scooby Gang, and also Willow's girlfriend. She is also a witch with magical powers and, in fact, is a very good influence for Willow in contrast to Amy. Incidents surrounding Tara's fate is what causes Willow to go berserk as Dark Willow. She was played by Amber Benson
Warren Mears	Unquestionably the evilest and the leader of the supervillain nerd group the Trio. Warren is a violent and egoistic technology expert in the trio. He is also the one who usually leads the trio on their various villainous escapades. He shoots Buffy and is responsible for shooting Tara as well (the spoiler I tried to avoid in the book). He is eventually killed by Dark Willow. He was played by Adam Busch

(*Continued*)

Name	Brief Description
Wesley Wyndham-Pryce	Wesley is another Watcher, who was appointed as Buffy and Faith's new Watcher, but proved to be ineffective due to his pomposity. While not a great success in BtVS, Wesley did find a much bigger part in the spinoff series, *Angel*. He was played by Alexis Denisof
Willow Rosenberg/Dark Willow	Willow is Buffy's best friend at Sunnydale, and initially a shy and unsure studious girl, but who goes on to become one of the most powerful witches in the entire series. She also goes through an antagonist phase when she becomes the primary antagonist in season 6 as Dark Willow. She was played by Alyson Hannigan
Xander Harris	Xander is another of Buffy's best friends at Sunnydale, and a primary member of the Scooby Gang. A wisecracking witty and loyal dependable friend throughout the series. He is also engaged to Anya but ends up not going through with the marriage due to his own insecurities. He was played by Nicholas Brendan

INDEX

www.ingramcontent.com/pod-product-compliance
Lightning Source LLC
Chambersburg PA
CBHW061255220326
41599CB00028B/5667